SIMPLE SYSTEMS, COMPLEX ENVIRONMENTS

MANAGING INFORMATION

A Series of Books in Organization Studies and Decision-Making

Edited by **AARON WILDAVSKY,** *University of California, Berkeley*

> What impact does the computer have on organizations (both public and private), and the individual decision makers within them?
>
> How can "data" be converted into "information for decision"?
>
> Who produces (and who consumes) such data? with what effects? under which conditions?
>
> What are the sources of error—and the means of overcoming them—in contemporary management information systems (MIS)?
>
> What is the state of the art in MIS theory?
>
> How can we increase our understanding of information and its management, as well as the surrounding organizational environment?

These are critical questions in an era of information overload, coupled with the need for decision-making by managers and policy makers dealing with finite resources. The **Managing Information** series meets the need for timely and careful analysis of these vital questions. Studies from a variety of disciplines and methodological perspectives will be included. The series will analyze information management from both public and private sectors; empirical as well as theoretical materials will be presented.

Volume 2
MANAGING INFORMATION:
A Series of Books in Organization Studies
and Decision-Making

Series Editor: **AARON WILDAVSKY**

MARI MALVEY

SIMPLE SYSTEMS, COMPLEX ENVIRONMENTS

HOSPITAL FINANCIAL INFORMATION SYSTEMS

 **SAGE** PUBLICATIONS   Beverly Hills   London

For information address:

SAGE Publications, Inc.
275 South Beverly Drive
Beverly Hills, California 90212

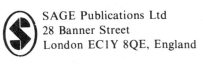

SAGE Publications Ltd
28 Banner Street
London EC1Y 8QE, England

Printed in the United States of America

Library of Congress Cataloging in Publication Data

Malvey, Mari.
   Simple systems, complex environments.
   (Managing information ; v. 2)
   Bibliography: p.
   1. Hospitals—Finance—Data processing. 2. Information storage and retrieval systems—Hospitals. 3. Management information systems. I. Title. II. Series.
RA971.6.M34   362.1'1'0681   80-29597
ISBN 0-8039-1541-1
FIRST PRINTING

09/20/82 – 17.50

CONTENTS

FOREWORD

LOOKED AT IN THE LARGE, organizations exist to suppress data. Some data are screened in, but most are screened out. The very structure of organization — the units, the levels, the hierarchy — is designed to reduce data to manageable and manipulable proportions. If top executives were willing and able to sift through all the booming and buzzing confusion themselves — to enjoy, like Haroun Al Rascheed, unmediated access to the primary sources — there would be no need for a "lowerarchy" or, indeed, for organization itself. Instead, at each level, there is not only compression of data but absorption of uncertainty. It is not the things in themselves but data-reduction summaries that are passed up until, at the end, executives are left with mere chains of inferences. Whichever way they go, error is endemic: If they seek original sources, they are easily overwhelmed; if they rely on what they get, they are easily misled.

The rise of modern management information systems (MIS) has both alleviated and aggravated the organizational dilemma inherent in having too much random data in the world and too little ordered information in organization. At the simplest levels, involving clear goals and calculable resources,

like writing checks, the ever-increasing capacities of computer-
ization have relieved organizations of much drudgery as both
volume and control become compatible. At more complex
levels, where objectives are multiple, contradictory, and vague,
and calculability is uncertain or absent; the capacity to produce
more data at lower cost per bit is stultifying. Just as mountains
are climbed because they are there, more data are produced
because it is possible. The quota of data enhancement is over-
fulfilled. But the task of data reduction becomes harder all the
time. The chance that collectable data will be missed goes
down, but the probability they will be lost or misinterpreted
goes up. At the heart of the difficulties over MIS is the built-in
tension between organizational structure designed to divide
and the MIS designed to multiply data.

In any organization, formal information systems exist side
by side with informal personal networks. No formal system is
likely to tell the user where to get additional data or what would
be relevant to current concerns. What to believe often depends
on whom to trust. As a general rule, formal systems should be
more reliable and informal systems should be speedier. Enter,
then, automated MIS: more data about more subjects. Now
there are possibilities of knowing something about more matters: the number and range of decisions increase, but the time
available to consider a single decision decreases either because
more levels are necessary to interpret the data or because of an
increase in possible decisions. As the number of levels times
the number of decisions at each level increases arithmetically,
the number of data-reduction summary inferences increases
geometrically. Validity is called into question. Thus, the increase in computing capacity in the formal system has the
paradoxical effect of encouraging greater use of the informal
apparatus.

As there are more decisions to make and more data about
each of them, with less time for assessment, decision makers
become concerned that they may have missed something;
perhaps something left out inadvertently or deliberately summarized out of the MIS. Not knowing exactly what they need,

which depends on emerging events, executives are tempted to order more. Why be half safe? Besides, each new set of data may provide a check on the others related to it. Alas, each new set also raises questions about the others, for if each were accurate why would they not say the same thing? Does MIS speak (or has it been misinterpreted to speak) with a forked tongue? Swamped by data, having even less time than before, managers require means of interpretation that are both speedier and more specific. They need to know what is reliable and right in a shorter time frame. So they ask around. Thus, they end up making more use of both formal and informal systems.

People in organizations generally overestimate the extent of simplicity in the organization's environment. There is a tendency to assume that one's description of a task or process is shared, that understanding is readily transported across boundaries and levels without losses in meaning, and that rules and regulations can be worked out to cover most situations and made binding on organization members. Actually, an organization's environment is only partially described, and then only, depending on one's perspective. Codes and rules constantly break down as things change or as people change their ideas about what is needed at a given time and in a given place. Consequently, management information systems are generally "neater" and more static than the organizations for which they are designed.

Why do intelligent people engage in fixing the faults of management information systems, only to fix them over and over again? Why do they fail in the first place to install systems that convert bits of data into information that makes a difference to what is decided, let alone into knowledge that directs them to the desired result? Why, beyond regular and routine chores, where objectives are crystal clear and resources exceed requirements, do these systems fail to provide accurate information for management? Why is this failure ordinary rather than exceptional? What might be done to overcome these difficulties?

The Managing Information series is designed to answer these two questions: 1. Why are there epidemics of error? 2. How might their frequency be reduced? Two types of error might be mentioned: perverse incentives and maximizing in opposite directions. Both are rooted in inadequate understanding of the social, organizational context within which MIS are placed.

The perverse structure of incentives among the organizations within which MIS are located, incentives that punish decrease in data but do not reward additions to information, constitute the main causes of failure. If data addition rather than data reduction is reasonable, then the behavior about which there is so much complaint — overload of overburdened executives — represents rational behavior.

Put baldly, attempting to maximize along opposing vectors is a no-no for students of resource allocation as well as logic. Given certain well-known boundary conditions, for instance, creating human beings who are maximally high and wide is not "on". Creating information systems that serve as many different users and/or purposes as possible at lower cost than any one alone is an article of faith, almost the very definition of the efficiency advantages of MIS. Yet, what is this but another doomed effort at mutual maximization? Still, embracing rather than avoiding this contradiction (squaring the circle of MIS, so to speak, as if it were virtuous instead of vacuous) is responsible for failures of function as well as excesses in cost.

The concrete manifestation of these rather abstract principles occurs every day. I expect it occurs somewhere in this country almost all the time, when someone discovers that hotbed of inefficiency and harbinger of opportunity, overlap and duplication. Within this worrisome organization are numerous units, all (or many or most) of which have their own MIS, including overlapping functions and duplicated questionnaires. This will not do. Imagine the savings that would flow from having a single MIS with a single questionnaire and a single set of programs run through a single set of machines. Perhaps, if this is done well, generality has been achieved. But what about power?

Mari Malvey has investigated this relationship in the context of billing by two hospitals in which seemingly simple systems had disintegrated into something resembling a cross between fourteenth-century flagellants and Charlie Chaplin's *Hard Times*. The right people did not get the correct bills. Many more machines were added but the MIS only made more mistakes. Indeed, the hospitals would have collapsed for lack of green stuff, were it not for the fact that bootlegging and parallel systems actually kept the cash coming. Why, she wondered, did what was previously considered information become data? Why did a system good for everyone in general turn out to be bad for anyone in particular? Because generality and particularity cannot be maximized, they must, instead, be compromised if the one is not to be the enemy of the other.

Let us look at the record. Under the old, inefficient system, each unit was largely independent of the others. It kept its own schedule, followed its own rules, made its own priorities. Praise or blame could be assessed and traced to its source. Duplication, overlap and redundancy vastly reduced the need for coordination. Time mattered within units but not between them. Status differences between units were neutralized insofar as their effects on MIS were concerned. All this changed with the bigger, but not better, MIS. Each unit was responsible for a portion of the new general-purpose form, which had to pass through all units within a certain time and in the specified order. Lateness in one unit ramified throughout the others. Status differentials were magnified. How could the billing unit coerce the medical unit, which was too busy saving lives to push papers? Coordination changed from automatic to apocalyptic. One need go no further, then, to suggest that just as there is a price for particularity, there is a cost for generality, and that these must be considered in view of local circumstances (who can get whom to do what, how soon, and how well).

Other books in this series will deal with different aspects of converting data into information for decision-making. Each will be based on detailed empirical work in organizations, so the reader can see who produces and who consumes data, with what effect, and under what conditions. Each will also address both the sources of error and the means of overcoming them. From time to time I shall attempt to cut across these and other studies by building a body of theory that codifies the state of the art. We hope that our understanding of information will grow with our knowledge of the organizations in which they are embedded.

— Aaron Wildavsky

INTRODUCTION

THE PROBLEMS OF IMPLEMENTING a computerized MIS are for the most part nontechnical. The major problems are linking these systems to the behavior of participants and embedding them within the organizational structure. Making a management information system work often required greatly simplifying, smoothing, or leaving out parts of an organization. In addition, other parts cannot be described precisely, or they may resist description altogether. The difficulty is that the oversimplified but "working" model of organizational life may be taken for the real thing. Furthermore, the new description requires new behavioral rules that people in the organization are unwilling to accept.

Two medium-sized nonprofit, voluntary general hospitals installed management information systems for the purpose of financial control. Both hospitals were familiar with simple data-processing at the accounting and payroll levels. Both hospitals proceeded in the time-honored fashion, stating objectives, appointing a committee to coordinate the project, and systematically evaluating each alternative before finally settling on a reasonable choice. A year after the implementation, however, neither hospital had a management information system capable of generating information for financial decision-making at management levels. Both hospitals had, instead, essentially transaction-processing and summary systems that showed little promise of evolving into information systems that could be used at different administrative levels, let alone becoming "total" hospital information systems, as their proponents had hoped. The hospitals themselves were astonished at their lack of success: How was it possible to go wrong with an essentially simple system? When we study the history of these two information systems, it becomes clear that neither the effect on interpersonal relationships nor the impact of a management information system was understood before the information system was installed. What system designers had seen as a simple financial management system was simple on the drawing boards, but it lost its simplicity when it was applied to a complex organization. Neither hospital understood how powerful a determining force the organization's highly involved network of relationships and rapidly changing environment would have on the MIS. In ignoring or misreading the critical determinants, each hospital was led to oversimplify the complexity with which the organization functioned. The importance of the delicate balance the organization manages between its public and private lives, its complicated process of negotiation among different sectors as a means of maintaining order, its deliberate cultivation of multiple objectives and multiple points of view as error control strategies, were not taken into consideration in system design. The result was that the hospital was linked together through a major, formal information channel which caused additional work for people and exacerbated status differences, because the administrative sector could not coerce medical units to complete paperwork. Lateness in one unit affected all others. As the demands of multiple users at various levels were made known, changes were constantly added to the system, but so general-purpose were these changes that few people could benefit. Distributing the same reports to everyone meant that few were able to use them without converting information back into data! Fortunately, what kept the hospitals functioning financially was that people who had to work with the system invented novel ways to get around it. Those at other levels of the organization ignored the output and relied on parallel or mostly informal information as well as experience-tied problem-solving strategies.

Interviews with personnel of both hospitals form the basis for this book. The experiences of the two hospitals — they are here treated as one hospital because each encountered the same problems — point to some significant tradeoffs that need to be made in complex environments when management information systems are intended. These tradeoffs relate to generality and power, to error and complexity, to risk and uncertainty, and to rationality and incentive systems.

Failing to understand properly the nature of tasks and functions performed by different managerial groups, or to provide strategies to accommodate for different and potentially conflicting aims, resulted in *overly reduced* system assumptions. This created low quality data, because no incentives existed to make them anything else. Not knowing what to collect led to *overcollection,* because the large, general model was unresponsive to learning and theory development, and consequently it could not explain what was necessary to decision making and what was not. The result was error. The failure to understand the necessity of deliberately engineered feedback mechanisms to permit trial-and-error learning in order to build knowledge resulted in *overdistribution* of data that did not contain policy-relevant variables and therefore did not aid decision-making. Failure to locate information relevant to each decomposable unit increased the uncertainty of task environments. The consequence of failing properly to decompose decision-making into the appropriate task- and problem-solving capabilities resulted in *interconnected systems.* Interconnected systems are difficult to control, because of conflicting objectives, needs, and costs. As a result, systems become inflexible and unresponsive to their environments.

Overreduction, overcollection, overdistribution, and interconnection are expensive consequences. A vastly overextended MIS represents an inefficient and ineffective allocation of resources. The system is ineffective in that there is no way to discover what approaches "optimal" in data, and it is inefficient because collecting, storing, updating, and retrieving costs are high. The costs of change in the form of adaptations are high, and the costs of error are also high. The costs of getting, storing, and maintaining the data collection are all functions of the data base. If the organization has limited resources, the more data are collected, the more changes in the system are necessitated, and the more tenuous is the fit between data and decision, the fewer will be the resources available for other uses.

1 Hospital Environments

A HOSPITAL HAS FEW characteristics which find exact parallels in business firms. The structure itself, the multiplicity of professional viewpoints, the effects of status, are not easily accommodated within profit-seeking firms. Even the number of actors capable of influencing hospital policy would create chaos in business firms. The dilemma for hospitals is that efficient management requires the use of business techniques and strategies. The organization proceeds in the face of obstacles to the contrary, both inside and out of the hospital. However, the very nature of organizational constraints — the impact of public influence upon the hospital, the two value systems, the differences between individual and organizational goals, and the pattern of investments at different levels of the hospital organization — all require a management that is left deliberately unstructured at certain levels in order to assimilate conflict over goals and make it possible for the two value systems of fiscal efficiency and health care to work together in relative harmony.

A management information system designed to become a total hospital information system may exclude critical data that reflect the system's complexity and undermine the information system's effectiveness. Further, the information system may be unable to handle data about certain organizational goals, such as quality, and leave out this data altogether, vastly oversimplifying the organization and causing the information produced in the MIS to be judged inadequate for decision-making.

THE EXTERNAL ENVIRONMENT

The hospital is subject to two sets of operational impacts from external sources (Garrett, 1973: 66): restrictions and demands. Restrictions may be placed upon the hospital by government agencies, professional organizations, or public groups. These restrictions may take the form of limitations upon activities. In this way, hospitals are not permitted expansion, new service areas, or the acquisition of certain capital-intensive medical equipment. They may take the form of standards or conditions of licensure and accreditation, of contracts or obligations to medical staffs or patients. Increasingly, however, the largest area of constraint is economic, in that hospitals have to conform to strict reimbursement guidelines laid down by government authorities and, in addition, establish a public and neutral set of criteria by which their activities are audited, to assure the public that it is in fact getting what it pays for. Accordingly, a heavy load is placed upon the financial management, as well as medical management, of the hospital to meet increased reporting requirements imposed by government agencies and insurance carriers.

The second set of operational impacts comes from demands from the community at large. Hospitals are asked to meet the needs for services that increasingly fit into the definition of "total health care," despite the fact that they are more exactly structured to fit the needs of short, acute care. People expect to find services ranging from dental to weight or habit control, diet and exercise, and public health education. Accordingly, health services have expanded and grown more expensive in recent years, as public demand as well as changing technology have been assimilated. Increased impingement from the outside, however, has caused hospitals to search for greater and more effective strategies to balance the conflict between greater demand and fewer resources. These strategies show that there is a distinction of "fundamental character" between the public life and the private life of the organization. The public life consists of public discussion and government decision about the financing, organization, regulation, and structure of the medical care delivery system. The private life is what actually happens in the day-to-day activities of people engaged in health care. While these two lives are of necessity connected, these connections are usually problematic. Moreover, the pressures of the public life, often expressed in demands for greater accountability and control, tend to stress one aspect of the organization over others; as a result, the readily quantifiable, transferrable data of performance are easily picked up. However, without the mediation of far less quantifiable data on quality and standards of performance, these data could be meaningless.

PRIVATE AND PUBLIC AIMS

What all institutions have in common today is a distinction between their "public" lives and their "private" ones, between what is supposed to happen and what actually does happen in their real lives. Martin Trow (1975) has provided an insightful clue to the consequences of the widening separation between the private and public lives of an institution in his studies of universities. "Tension," Trow reports, " increases when people who are far-removed from the institution's private life are allowed to make decisions without regard for their real consequences for the organization's private life." This growing "publicness," as Trow sees it, can strongly influence the internal decision-making and the character of the data systems intended to provide information. Trow goes on to note that administrators feel they cannot be unresponsive to what appear to be perfectly legitimate calls for better and more information on how institutions spend public funds, but that there are risks for the institution involved as well.

On one hand, administrators have an interest in developing better data systems that along with other information will enable them to make more defensible decisions about resource allocations, as well as achieve better control over the collection and deployment of those resources. On the other hand, they must be prepared to respond to "continual demands from the government for more information." The dilemma for the administrative sector is that it may well be sensitive to the private needs and private life of the hospital; however, any information it turns up for its own use may, sooner or later, find its way into the files of external agencies. Clearly describing where the organization is doing well and where it is not, for example, could be volatile information in the hands of the wrong agencies. For this reason, Trow concludes that the "costs to the organization of new and improved internal data systems may be rather higher than originally anticipated." One hospial administrator agreed, noting that "we have to tell the government everything. But why? No more than 2 percent of the examiners are hospital-experienced or can adequately understand our situation. If we make a savings today, they think, good, you can do even better tomorrow. They fail to realize that what we save for them we have to make up elsewhere in the structure if there's a cost to be borne."

Tensions inevitably escalate between such public goals as accountability and equity on one hand, and balanced budgets on the other, and lead to uneasy relations. Hospitals bemoan the "suspicious and mistrustful nature of the government. They seem more interested in catching the few rip-off artists than they are in genuine cost-control. As a result, the rest of us get penalized. You have no idea how much it costs us to turn out these reports." One of the more publicized episodes of the public-private conflict is contained in the furor over utilization review, where hospitals are mandated to organize medical committees to develop and supervise the implementation of care criteria in the treatment of illness, and to carry out studies and document their findings on utilization of care facilities. The government cites overwhelming cost, which has forced it to look to standardization and guidelines to bring costs into line. Doctors, on the other hand, refer to utilization review as an attempt to usurp their authority, "a blatant attempt to dictate sub-standard care."

Another official referred to the increased public involvement in medical expenditure and demands for greater accountability in the use of resources as "an unending dilemma. . . . The public says, cut here. We do. Then another public rises up and says no, don't you dare, it's not in the 'public interest' to cut there. We find ourselves between the 'devil and the deep blue sea' if we have anything on paper that says, here's a place to cut down on expenses." Therefore, it is in the interests of the hospital and its strategically located participants to refuse to accept definitions of objectives that put them at a disadvantage or proscribe future courses of action.

Furthermore, accountability and equity may be goals that conflict in practice. An administrator mentioned that a special clinic had recently been added to the hospital which "is actually a money-loser now, but a lot of people were very vocal that it would serve the needs of a neglected minority (old people). The medical staff opposed it for some time, but they were finally overcome. . . . We had to add it if we were to fulfill our obligations to the community. Yet there is no consensus among the medical group that this type of service does any good at all, or that it comes anywhere near attacking the real problems of older people. A lot of people out there want it anyway."

Not only external agencies and quasi-public authorities are involved in the search for equity and accountability. There is a multiplicative effect that reaches to other bodies — professional organizations, employee unions, insurance carriers, and so forth. Data developed for the use of one agency may turn up elsewhere, where they are received as antagonistic, adding to the bewildering array of public aims struggling for expression, aims that may be perceived as counter to individual interests or merely undefinable.

Still another important aspect of the public/private dilemma concerns the nature of "public " data. These data may only be data that are easily quantified, such as numbers of procedures per day, per unit, or whatever, while soft data, which are difficult to quantify or which resist translation across boundaries, do not find their way into the public channel. What, for example, is quality of care? How does one specialty define health as opposed to another specialty or group of professionals? What constitutes good care? These are questions that vitally concern the organization and its financial future, but they are not easily addressed within the public information system. Unfortunately, when only quantitative indicators are addressed by a MIS, however, the meaning of the data may be jeopardized without an understanding of how good or how bad the delivery of service is. Knowing the number of treatments per technician per day, or of patients served per specialty, may not be useful for planning purposes unless planners know if the hospital is doing a good job or a poor job of delivery. The result, however, is important to the hospital's resource base.

DUAL VALUE SYSTEMS

The hospital makes effective use of the principles of "local" rationality, incorporated in the idea of dual authority systems that reflect the value orientations of medicine and business efficiency, as well as accountability for services performed in the name of those values. Medical treatment concerns itself with treating patients, not primarily with the cost of treatment, leaving that problem to financial administrators. In this way, ethical considerations are protected against the use of the pragmatics or economics as a criterion of choice. Adminstrators have a sense of duty to the doctors and patients who use the hospital, but they resign the articulation of the specific processes by which care is accomplished in the medical sector. The medical sector can leave problems of efficiency, cost containment, and service volume to the adminstrative sector. One method by which both sets of concerns are enabled to live side by side is to suppress precise articulations of goals to lower and lower organizational levels, so that there is room for multiple views, since people within the organization have different views about the proper function of the hospital. Simon and March (1959) suggest that differences over organizational goals may be due to differences in patterns of interaction among members. In fact, the substance of organizational theory from Weber on argues for the predominance of "private agendas" in the organization rather than consensus on goals. Ackoff notes that the conflicting measures of performance used to judge departments may not improve communication, but may actually work counter to the organization's interests. In short, subgoal formation and goal conflict are significant features of organizational life.

In the hospital, different sectors, different levels, and different personnel may share only a single vague and ambiguous "charter goal" aimed at returning patients to the outside world in better shape. This goal acts as a symbol that permits all in the organization to work constitutionally, but it in fact masks considerable disagreement and discrepant purpose, which arises when goals are made explicit and specific.

Making objectives specific might be seen by some members as closing off options. For example, since "medicine is only partially and imperfectly related to health," there is considerable uncertainty in the medical system. One way it deals with uncertainty is by holding all options open as long as possible. If one follows Wildavsky's (1977: 104) Medical Uncertainty Principle, there is "always one more thing that might be done — another consultation, a new drug, a different treatment" that might resolve particular cases of uncertainty, "the doctor . . . ordering more services, the patient . . . requesting more."

Thus, if medical uncertainty suggests that existing services will be used, the Identity reminds us to add the words "up to

available supply." That supply is primarily doctors, who advise on the kind of care to be sought, the number of hospital
beds (only one person in a bed at a time), and the number of
patients making demands.

To doctors, then, uncertainty is countered "efficiently" by
doing as much as possible for patients. Medical efficiency is in
turn countered with social efficiency, which attempts to set cost
controls on treatment.

As individual patients are encountered by the organization's
actors, the generalized mandate expires and each actor views the
patient as unique within a highly uncertain therapy. Almost everyone considers himself the principal agent for bringing about improvement in the patient's condition. However, what constitutes
improvements, and how these improvements should be pursued,
is far from clear, and not every member of the organization
believes that financial efficiency ultimately contributes to the
general good, to the overall goal of good patient care, or even to
the individual therapeutic goals of individual patients. From the
start, then, there is a basis for conflict in the delivery of health care
services. Much of this conflict can be attributed to the types of
investments and commitments the principal actors in the hospital
make at different organizational levels.

ORGANIZATIONAL OBJECTIVES

In the hospital, heterogeneity of purpose and function combined with considerable decentralization of authority make for
increased goal proliferation. There are a number of actors with
general goals at one level, with overlapping goals at another,
but with often conflicting goals at the level of the specific unit
or department.

In terms of policy influence, there are major groupings of
individuals — nurses, medical staff, unions — who express
their interests legitimately. In addition, however, there are sig-

nificant, but smaller, groups of "strategically placed elites" who ignore official groupings to articulate interests or else are sought out by the hospital administration because of the authority or status they possess, or their ability to influence policy. There are conflicts of interest among major influencers. Garrett (1973: 68), for example, has pointed out that, unlike business firms, makers of organization policy as well as implementers of this policy are often the same persons.

Let us consider the principal actors in the hospital.[1]

The board of directors sees the hospital as a community resource committed to the provision of quality medical care, as defined largely by the doctors and implemented by the administrator. The board expects to intervene in, influence, or even manage the setting of policies which concern the distribution of the hospital's resources or the quality of its care, for which the board holds final responsibility.

The board is charged with the ultimate responsibility for all aspects of the hospital. It must decide questions of organization, personnel, funds, and allocations of resources, as well as oversee the efficient management of the hospital. Because it is removed from the day-to-day activities of the hospital, the board may choose to concern itself with articulating the central purpose and responsibility of the hospital and leave many aspects of the actual operation to the discretion and skill of the administrator acting as its surrogate. The board is conscious of its obligation to be an effective governing body for the hospital, however.

The administrator sees himself or herself as the coordinator of a complex managerial enterprise that must meet broadly defined community goals as well as produce a quality product under conditions of sound fiscal management.

The administrator represents the board of directors, but is also interested in influencing policy. Because of the number of demands for funds and their scarcity, the administrator is engaged in ongoing analysis of existing conditions, mobilizing resources and applying these resources to specified ends. The administrator is generally the only hospital manager able, by training and experience, to adopt a comprehensive view of the institution.

The physicians see themselves as the final arbiters in clinical decisions and view the hospital as the facilitator of whatever they may demand in the name of their patients. The medical staff generates the income for both the hospital and its major expenses, yet it does not work directly for the hospital, instead officially operating outside the administrator's authority as guests of the institution. Doctors voluntarily adapt to constraints imposed by the medical staff, the hospital, and third party agreements. When doctors become department managers, they become responsible for the organization and management of their departments, the medical care of patients treated within those departments, and the enforcement of hospital rules. While they may become part of the administration, they may not be paid employees of the hospital.

The ancillary professional staff expects to participate in the areas of their expertise on decisions affecting both the patient and the functioning of the hospital. Professionals may or may not be paid employees of the hospital, but they expect to influence budgets on behalf of their departments and the patients they serve. Professionals subscribe to canons and standards prescribing behavioral practices. They will not hesitate to intervene in established policy or authority relationships if they believe the circumstances of patients warrant it.

The department of financial services is under increasing pressure from forces within as well as outside of the hospital to provide rigorous documentation of and accounting for how the hospital spends its money and deploys its resources.

Within the same organization, some individuals are advocates for individuals, as are doctors, while others are advocates for groups of individuals, as are the administrator and the board. Some create income for the organization, as the doctors and professional departments do, while others, like the department of financial service, must justify that income to agencies like the federal government, which require very explicit and detailed explanations of what they are paying for.

All these actors expect in one way or another to influence the information passing through the organization. In order to keep these competing interests and viewpoints balanced enough to permit organizational life to function, the hospital makes use of intricate negotiation strategies. These will be discussed in the next chapter to show how frequently integration is restored and change assimilated by strategies that resist articulation in macro-organizational terms.

A HOSPITAL MIS

Not only did the hospital fail to realize and plan for its complexity as an organization, it failed to perceive the diversity and conflict of objectives within the financial accounting system. The hospital wanted a comprehensive, totally integrated, automated MIS, capable of providing financial reporting, accounting, and planning data:

(1) It would have a detailed data base for use of billers and those who compiled the appropriate billing reports.

(2) It would have access to accounting that utilized, summarized, and aggregated data for reports at that level.

(3) It would have data suitable for summarizing and analyzing financial performance in statements and various planning documents for internal and external purposes.

(4) It would have the capability of performing utilization reviews, auditing patient care performance, and reporting appropriately.

(5) It would have data to aid in the choice of strategies to advance the hospital's financial growth and development over the long term.

These capabilities would be serially connected: Data output from billing would input into accounting, which in turn would become the input of financial planning. All sections would be built upon the base of detailed data, and there would be a multitude of subprograms and subsections that would deal with such activities as reporting revenue, reporting insurance category performance, reporting productivity, reporting income and analyzing cash pictures, and singling out trends impacting the hospital.

Multiple data banks would be contained in the system: (1) patient information, (2) accounts receivable, (3) patient records, medical records, and utilization review, (4) personnel, (5) financial reporting, and (6) general accounting.

HOW DID THE HOSPITAL PROCEED?

The hospital saw the management information system as the solution to problems originating both inside and outside the organization. From the external environment there were growing pressures for documentation and verification of cost-cutting measures in government-financed accounts, as well as for increased systematization and procedural compliance from third-party payers in general. There were demands for services from different community groups as well as demands for additional technology and specialized staff within the hospital's existing service units. There was also increased awareness of the quality of hospital care and interest on the part of the public in holding the hospital accountable for the quality of services delivered by specialists within the organization. Furthermore, the hospital's management desired to take advantage of opportunities for new revenues available within an affluent and health-oriented community.

THE RESULT

In attempting to develop a comprehensive system for financial control, the hospital took an essentially complicated organizational environment and made it more complicated.

(1) It ignored the complex considerations surrounding a multi-plicity of conceivable objectives, hedged in by numerous constraints of purpose, value, and direction of effort.

(2) It attempted to reduce all these goals and values to those of public, quantifiable, efficiency.

(3) It took a system of financial accounting and control that was innately disparate and potentially conflicting and tried to merge all functions into one interconnected and interdependent channel.

The MIS assumed that everyone had the same objective and that this objective was financial efficiency. Yet, even within the financial accounting function, there is little commonality on objectives, since different organizational levels address different purposes. The billing staff is concerned that *individual* patients are adequately serviced; another level is concerned that *groups* of patients are adequately serviced; another level is interested in fulfilling certain fiscal reporting requirements that are imposed upon the organization. At still another level, the concern is not with these requirements, but with their consequences: If the government pays x for a given procedure and the actual cost to the hospital is x plus, how is the additional amount to be absorbed by the hospital? Still another level wants to know about the cumulative effects of a number of consequences: Where are we going? Are we doing better or worse?

THE IMPLICATIONS FOR A MIS

The hospital is a complicated setting with many objectives and no easy or convenient method to separate them. Moreover, it may not be preferable to do so, since they all contribute to the delivery of a highly complex and uncertain product — health. In general, these aims reduce both definition and explication. A MIS that selects some, but not all, for expression could seriously jeopardize the delicate balance which makes the delivery of medical services within an organizational setting a reality. At the very least, the system will be ignored by many medical components.

The organization proceeds in the face of innumerable obstacles stemming from the different patterns of investment at different levels of the hospital. Nevertheless, it does proceed. Proceeding strictly on the basis of public criteria and public data alone is unrealistic, in view of the fact that public data are generally data that can be expressed by quantitative indicators and that might be meaningless without the mediation of private data to express quality.

Even though medical care and the administration of medical care are separate systems, the financial management of the hospital entails both sectors and is by no means simple and straightforward just because numbers are involved. When the different dimensions of efficient and effective financial management — medical, administrative, private, public, individual-advocate, group-advocate — are added together, the picture of financial administration grows enormously. For example, groups within the community want the hospital to add or delete certain services, while the hospital, insofar as it can affect the ordering of what it delivers, wants to produce services that pull their own weight. The government wants the costs of delivery, if not curtailed, at least contained, while doctors claim the only criterion they are willing to adhere to is what is best for individual patients, since they know they will be reimbursed anyway. Conflict exists between levels of decisions for data appropriate to one purpose and levels inappropriate to another.

If these many facets of the organization and its goals are not adequately described within the MIS, then it will not be a valid picture of the organization, and it will not increase predictability for decision makers. When the hospital installed its MIS, it failed adequately to consider these basic constraints.

NOTE

1. For a discussion of management in the hospital, see Gordon (1961-1962).

2 Factors in Coordinating the Hospital

TWO SETS OF PARALLEL relationships characterize the hospital organization: the informational and the behavioral. The internal informational relationship runs vertically through the hospital in two directions: upward, as generated by the physician-nurse-patient triad, and downward, through policy formulations originated by the administrator and the board of directors (Howland, 1961).

All units in the hospital are activated by the flow of data through the hospital. As data are collected, stored, and distributed, they set in motion the action premises constituting each unit's function and contribution to patient care. Data flow downward from the top of the organization. First, as a means of calibrating and recalibrating the busy internal channel, it sends signals: "Hurry up, we're moving too slowly." "Costs are out of line." "Too many people are working overtime." The second purpose of the downward flow of information is to stabilize, by interpreting or minimizing the impact of the external environment upon the hospital organization. This is accomplished through long-range plans with a view to such matters as increasing population, increasing health care demands, rapid changes in technology, the appearance of new competition, and public demands for cost accountability.

The behavioral relationship runs parallel to the informational, but does not necessarily coincide with it. Many different behavioral sectors — medical, professional, administrative — some dealing with patient care, others only indirectly, coexist in the hospital. There is little or no relationship between the different sectors, nor does there need to be, on a continuing basis, for the departmental organization is one emphasizing self-sufficiency and independence.

In most institutions, planning and control are effected by bringing the informational relationship into congruence with the behavioral. In the hospital organization, coordination is achieved first by the assurance that the primary units are norm-governed and sustain their behavior internally on an ongoing basis. Coordination among units is achieved by use of information as well as strategies like rule-avoidance and negotiation to mediate the information passing busily through the information channel. It is a complex and delicate process, reflecting the complexity of the hospital organization, which enables the hospital constantly to recreate order out of chaos.

An important part of information system design is properly relating individuals and activities performed in the orgainization. Frequently, however, MIS designers overemphasize the static, orderly, and rule-governed elements of an organization, and underestimate the place of flux, seeming disorder, and rule avoidance in the organization's day-to-day activities. These elements are quite characteristic in the hospital organization and serve the purpose of permitting effective and rapid response to change. Accordingly, as procedures fluctuate in response to change in the organization's environment, disorder is both a strategy for rapid assimilation of change and a mechanism permitting the slack that is necessary to assimilate a multitude of theoretical perspectives. Rule-avoidance permits opportunities for self-directness when necessity demands rapid response.

PROFESSIONALS AND COORDINATION

The proliferation of specialist professionals has had important effects on the organization of medical care in hospitals. One effect noted by Heydebrand (1975: 124-129) is "the generalist form, as found in the traditional or administrative professions, may actually provide integration and coordination of specialized work functions and thus reduce procedural communications and supervisory enforcement of operative rules." Professionals, on the other hand, are themselves part of a system of the division of labor, especially when they are employees of an organization. Rather than contributing to coordination, they are likely to require additional coordination and administrative regulation. Professionalism "modifies" the structure of decision-making and of supervision, particularly the classic principle of "unity of command" and the degree of close supervision. Self-direction in decision-making describes in part what March and Simon termed coordination by feedback, or communication aimed toward adaptation in contingency situations.

An example of coordination by feedback is the role of professional nurses in the organization of patient care. Nurses combine professional and administrative functions in one role. A physician may order a series of tests or request a procedure for a patient, but it is the nursing staff that translates orders into implementation for other components. A nurse exercises a considerable amount of discretion in coordinating. These functions are not formally a part of the hierarchical structure above his or her level, but constitute an independent realm of decision-making, delegation of functions, and lateral or downward authority.

THE CONFLICT WITHIN

In Cyert and March's (1966) formulations, an organization is a coalition of separate individuals with diverse goals. Individuals comprise subunits whose behavior is coordinated within the subunit. Each unit consumes resources and has a direct effect on other units in the organiziation. "Basically," they argue, "most organizations most of the time exist and thrive with considerable latent conflict of goals. Except at the level of nonoperational objectives, there is no internal consensus. The procedures for resolving such conflict do not reduce all goals to a common dimension or even make them internally consistent."

Couched in organizational terminology, conflict in organizations is inevitable, for while there may be pressure toward joint decision-making, there may be differences among individual goals or individual perceptions of reality. Hence, the sharing of goals is a function largely of recruitment procedures as well as interaction patterns within the organization; i.e., goals are shared on suborganizational levels.

Within the medical care system, conflict can be perceived as one strategy for dealing with the uncertainty of medicine, in that it fragments the medical function into smaller and specialized units better suited to handling the responsibility as well as understanding it. In this way, as perspectives are multiplied, so too are the possibilities for perceiving error. Each professional claims an ethical responsibility to monitor, for the sake of the patient, the work of all other professionals. For example, the pharmacist reports that he "checks each prescription on a patient for its interactive effects with other medicines and is responsible for pointing out to doctors problems he believes may arise." A further aspect of the medical component of the hospital is its differentiation in terms of various characteristics of professionalism: education or preparation, internalization of norms, assumptions of responsibility, and, particularly important for information systems, assumption of discretion.

RULE-BREAKING

The authority systems in hospitals respect the rights of professionals to break rules when the demands of patient care so require. Effective response when the need arises is generally facilitated in the hospital by rule-breaking, rather then rule-adherence. That is because the values of good patient care take precedence over all other organizational needs. In the interests of patient care, the primary care staff can depart at will from the formal system of structures and roles. They easily break bureaucratic rules on behalf of their patients and make demands upon the organization's resources that would be considered unreasonable or unjust if other members made them. Professional departments require large amounts of support. Nurses are overburdened, "always behind in administrative work because we are short-staffed and busy. We depend on clerks a great deal to do the detail work. . . . Well, to tell you the truth, many of us resent any duties which take us away from our patients, such as administrative routines and all that paperwork."

A familiar example of rule-breaking is the crisis or emergency situation, where all normal routines and procedures are temporarily amended at the discretion of the therapeutic staff. In general, under pressure of necessity, nurses will raid other departments on weekends, act as pharmacists, supply keepers or maids. The good nurse is often one who, in an emergency, can lay hands on whatever is necessary to a patient's care. The nurse has valuable supplies stashed away against such an occasion, or knows just who in the organization is capable of bypassing the rules to get something or repair a necessary piece of equipment should an emergency jeopardize the care of his or her patients. Of course, all categories of personnel are adept at breaking or stretching rules whenever exigencies arise.

In a hospital organization, particularly in light of the high turnover of personnel, it would be impossible to know all the rules and rule-governed situations. Strauss and his associates note that in the psychiatric hospital they studied rules were often agreed upon and enforced for a short time, but later fell into disuse. In other circumstances, personnel called upon rules to obtain what they themselves wished or to protect themselves against certain demands of other organizational members. Rule-avoidance is generally supported by administrators who are also motivated by the belief that the care of patients requires a minimum of rules and a maximum of discretion and adaptation.

The professional staffs that produce the hospital's array of services bring to the organization specialized knowledge, a widely accepted value system and a propensity to resist regulation. How, then, does the organization reach agreements that permit the daily work to continue? Primarily through negotiation.

NEGOTIATION

Because of the great complexity as well as the variety within the organization, there is considerable reliance upon negotiation to unify the organization. Negotiation makes it possible to integrate patient and nonpatient activities, individual and group interests, and to provide the force to blend the permanent with the changing structures in such a way that stability obtains and there is predictability in response. Agreements must be negotiated, states Gordon (1962), because

> the elements stem from the power relationships, the control relationships and the alternatives available to each group in what can best be seen as a negotiated relationship and one constantly subject to renegotiation. They stem out of the alternative means of leverage and the amount of power behind that leverage that is available to each party involved in the negotiation. . . . Stated baldly, on a day to day basis, the voluntary general hospital corporation and its agents have no legal or organizational means of controlling the service that the hospital has been set up to render.

The Strauss et al. (1971) view looks at the hospital as not one organization but a coalition of many organizations, each with a different pattern of authority and social behavior. Doctors are essentially collegial associates whose pattern of self-government proceeds in strictly democratic form. Other professionals may be organized semicollegially, but with nominal authority resting in a chairperson. Doctors claim allegiance to their patients; professionals such as pharmacists or therapists to their professions. In addition, some departments are associated with the hospital by contractual arrangement, and others, like the dietary service, are subsidiaries of a larger, external corporation with multiple members. Even departments that are organized hierarchically, such as laboratory technology, may require considerable decentralization by function and specialty within the occupational structure. People such as those who specialize in the maintenance and repair of medical equipment are technically so specialized that their work could only be supervised by others in the same profession.

Negotiation enables different elements of the division of labor to get on with their daily work by prescribing the conditions by which patient care functions are integrated with nonpatient ones, so that whatever other values rise to the surface of the organization's attention, such as efficiency or economy, the process of negotiation acts to restore patient care values to ascendancy. If this did not happen, the organization could not proceed as a hospital; it would be a different organization.

Negotiation provides a vehicle for integrating individual interests with those of group demands. An example of this is in the division between those who look after the general interests of a community of patients and those who are advocates for specific patients. Here, nonmedical and medical interests must achieve a balance in goal-seeking behavior to enable the organization to withstand external pressures and internal changes. This focuses upon negotiation as an interactive process where the basis of social action must be continuously reconstituted.

What the hospital is from day to day is a social order, a combination of agreements, contracts, obligations, understandings, and working arrangements that extend across sectoral boundaries and implicate all the members of the organization, and that require continuous restructuring. The result is a complex relationship between the "daily negotiative process and a periodic appraisal process" (Strauss et al., 1971).

INFORMAL NETWORK

In an organization composed almost entirely of professionals, unwritten communication conducted through a number of channels facilitates integration of both present and future actions. Is there any way the considerable variety of this communication could be encompassed by an information system? Probably not, for incorporating sufficient variety would make the cost of the system prohibitive. In addition, the great value of the informal system is in its tacit nature. Stating the conditions explicitly would be problematic, since many defy measurement, or would lead to conflict with one or another authority and generally foster discord.

An important use of informal communication is in equilibrating and negotiating the various functions within the hospital. Informal communication can set limits on the system's ability to make demands, or the opposite, expand system limits to incorporate new and necessary demands. For example, increasing productivity in one instance involved increasing the number of procedures each technician performed. The administrator wanted "to squeeze them for a while so as to get 18 procedures per technician, a little better than the professional average, but quite a bit better than the local one. We needed to get more because new departments had opened and were putting a bind on that department. Well, the Chief Tech said, no, his people would do 16, because that's what their colleagues were doing and what they wanted to do. Well, we went back and forth for a while, and finally I went down and asked them if they'd try it for a few months and see how it worked out. They agreed to do 17."

The use of informal channels to communicate across ethical concerns is another example of how the organization is made to function smoothly. Each physician on the staff has an obligation to help generate income for the hospital. The administrator may note from productivity reporting that a certain doctor has not been doing much for the hospital lately: "Now I can't write him and tell him to start sending us more sick people; I have to rely on something more subtle. I usually eat in the doctors' dining room so that I have a chance to get closer to the doctors, and then I can work the conversation around to the point I want to make."

A similar and even more difficult administrative task is that of supervising, at least indirectly, the quality of care delivered in the hospital, since the hospital is responsible for the medical practice delivered in its organization. As its appointed authority, the administrator is directly charged with ensuring that care is of quality. If the administrator is not a physician himself, he is discouraged from exercising direct supervision of medical affairs. However, he must be in a position to receive or intercept important information about the quality of care that might, one way or another, affect the hospital's future.

To get the information of this type, the administrator must rely on his own intelligence apparatus. "I read the minutes of all medical committees, but besides the statistics, I have to be able to read between the lines. For example, a committee might make a reference to reviewing a doctor. Now no committee of doctors is going to commit in writing the identification of a doctor it might suspect of being incompetent. I go around and gossip with the doctors and eventually find out who it is, and what his problem is, and if we need to be concerned or not. In fact, about three to five percent of the medical staff are regularly and quietly monitored for one reason or another. Everyone knows who those individuals are, and if I didn't, I'd be out of a job, but you will not see the names of these men written anywhere." Quite clearly, if the administrator relied only upon the information contained in the formal system, he would not know very much about what was going on in the organization's subcomponents, and what is going on is crucial for the organization's survival.

The hospital may appear to be many and contradictory organizations, united only by the vaguest of mandates, where the professional members appear to outweigh in power the more generalist members of the organization. However, it is this very differentiation that in fact provides the basis for integration, in that no one member or unit is self-sufficient or independent from the others. The strategy of exchange also enables the organization to accommodate and facilitate diverse behavioral modes.

EXCHANGE

Exchange focuses upon the creation of reciprocity and a balance of obligations which allows heterogeneous elements of the organization to achieve viability. The theory of exchange examines the conditions which facilitate the creation and maintenance of productive interpersonal relations. When viewed in terms of exchange, the creation of viable relations is contingent upon the prospect that the relationship will provide each partner with an exchange of favorable proportion.

There is a "balancing" aspect to a successful exchange, in that participants receive "reinforcements" for interacting with one another, so these relationships are likely to be sustained. Yet, there is a need to maintain a favorable balance of obligations, and each partner must perceive he is getting something from the interaction or else he will lose interest.

When the exchange concept is applied to the task of coordination in hospitals, it means that while there are strong tendencies within the organization toward diversification, which have emerged in response to the increasingly specialized nature of health care, exchange is capable of providing a basis for narrowing the gap between professionals and administrators, provided the basic condition of exchange is honored: There must be a favorable balance of obligations. While no group can effectively achieve all its objectives, it is motivated to maximize its position by engaging in relationships, that is, by cooperating with other sectors. The administrative sector has increased in specialization; it also holds specialized data, resources, or knowledge that others in the organization do not possess but wish to have. The price of possession is cooperation, which is redressed at another time when the administrative sector wishes something from one of the hospital's other specialized components. Social exchange provides a vital integrating mechanism capable of mediating conflict at all levels in the organization.

EXCHANGE VERSUS COMPETITION

Exchange differs from competition, in that exchange relations occur among horizontally differentiated, unlike, yet interdependent units. Competition, on the other hand, occurs among like units that are primarily independent and hierarchically differentiated. Differentiation and integration in complex organizations sets the necessary condition for exchange relations: heterogeneity, a limited number of competitors, and imperfect knowledge. These conditions are the opposite of those required by competition and are manifested in the social interaction in organizations in which individuals or groups exchange various contributions for material and social benefits. The more differentiated are the tasks of complex organizational members, the more varied will be the product produced by each, and the less feasible the substitutionality of one product for another. In hospitals, for example, the cost and scarcity of talent preclude the inclusion of multiples of specialties: There is one nuclear medicine department, one pharmacy or emergency, for example.

The lack of homogeneity and partialness of function actually inhibits competition and restricts freedom of movement, because the different specialized departments are highly dependent upon the support and services of all other departments. Therapeutic care departments need laboratories and pharmacies and dieticians and housekeeping services and a range of inputs that would be prohibitively expensive if each had to be obtained independently on open, competitive markets. In addition, quality-control and safety standards would not be achieved with the same guarantee or at the same level that the total organization of the hospital is able to enforce, through coordination.

Since hospitals are organizations and the number of members is limited, specialists actually constitute too small a group to be independent competitors; the transactions of one member generally do affect the conditions of exchange. A medical specialist has only to order a treatment or procedure for a patient for a whole array of interdepartmental activity to be called forth. These activities are produced regularly, upon demand. There is no need for individual specialists to seek the support of their colleagues, unless they wish to do so. At the same time, there are too few, say, cardiologists on a hospital staff to make it practical for the patient "to shop around" for a better diagnosis. In any case, the collegial disposition of doctors in a hospital is more likely to find them in agreement than in competition with each other.

In short, departments, even individuals, in complex organizations offer a particular expertise whose availability is limited. Consequently, no one expert single department is capable of fulfilling the entire demand for data. Finally, there is imperfect knowledge on the part of exchangers of all the conditions involved, because the amount of knowledge different individuals possess varies from individual to individual and is not comparable, in strict equivalents, across specialty lines. In addition, this knowledge is in fact affected by the position individuals occupy in the organizational hierarchy. The most obvious example is the possession of a highly reputed diagnostician or surgeon on the hospital staff. There is no substitutability in terms of value for the "product" of that individual. At the same time, the status accorded to the surgeon or diagnostician in turn capitalizes, so to speak, the value of his or her "product," with the result that people treat him or her differently from the way they treat others in the organization.

STATUS

The social context of the transaction is profoundly affected by status relationships. A basic proposition of organization theory is that those who make the most essential contributions to organization maintenance have the greatest claim to superior status. In hospitals, not only do doctors typically make the greatest contributions, they also produce a product for which there are no substitutes. By virtue of their occupational status, doctors can exert influence upon the price of a product, the output of services and goods, and even upon the demand for services, if they can convince enough patients to use that service. The benefits other members of the hospital organization receive are contingent upon the contribuitions made by the medical specialists.

High status not only accrues to medical specialists by virtue of their expertise, but it is also accorded to them consensually by the rest of the organization, which recognizes the value of their contribution. As a consequence, medical specialists command large amounts of respect and compliance both as a reward for past behavior and as an incentive for future contributions. Status is in this respect like capital, but it is not expended in usage as long as the transactor retains a high position.

From the perspective of its professional elements, the hospital is quite varied. Moreover, it is quite disorderly in that each person is busily engaged in pursuit of his or her own specialty, under conditions which he or she seeks to maximize to favor that pursuit. The organization proceeds under the rulc of sets of behaviors and norms that were imported into the organization.

In fact, the hospital functions best when decision makers do not lose sight of their individual aims, for these myriad and conflicting objectives increase the options of decision and so promote safety. Because professionals refuse to submit, and indeed cannot submit, their objectives entirely to one formal authority of rule, daily activity proceeds by negotiation rather than formal, rule-governed communication. Negotiation not only provides for the least stressful integration of the multiple interests of the organization's actors, it is also the best way of adapting to change and external pressures from the environment because it permits the dynamic accommodation that blends the enduring permanent structure (stability) with the demands of ongoing daily tasks (change). Negotiation supplies the premises for the continuous reanimation of the hospital system.

The hospital has evolved both purposely and intuitively a number of respones to the problems of operating in an environment of stress, flux, and uncertainty. These responses are integral to its ability to perform with predictability. In the hospital organization, multiple viewpoints facilitate error detection and correction. Considerable fragmentation of task is a pragmatic response to the need to accept the inherent limitations of a tightly linked system. The additions of redundancies through professionals, whose knowledge extends a little beyond their own specialties, also facilitates both error control and equipotentiality, so that subsidiary parts can take over, even if less efficiently, the functions of a part that has been damaged.

A management information system is a cybernetic mechanism that must, in Ashby's (1961) words, have variety commensurate with its environment, to be effective. Many hospital information systems fail to take into consideration the relationship between information and behavior in the hospital, or to pay attention to the enormously complex responses that constitute routines, "SOPs," and the like. MIS frequently fail because they are not embedded in the organization's complexity. They fail also because they offer no inducements to cooperation or alternatives to the sensitive and effective mechanism of exchange, which make the organization work. Next, we will look at some of the implications of these failures in terms of the information system.

3 Getting Data into the System

A CLASSIC ORGANIZATIONAL problem is how to get other organizational units to place a priority on producing work your unit needs. Management information systems assume that by specifying that there shall be inputs into the system, units will produce when and where required. If a unit is unwilling or unable to produce, what mechanisms do consumers have to get the product?

Producing daily or weekly data about a department's activities should be viewed as an exchange function. In a typical business firm, the production of data for the organization's MIS carries a potential benefit, in that a department producing such data also hopes to receive information that can be employed to promote the department's profit-making capabilities.

In a hospital, however, the exchange relationship in data production is more in the nature of a public good than of a market function. One department, the department of financial services, performs a service, the billing and collecting of money owed to the hospital, which benefits the hospital as a total entity, but which promotes no one unit over another. Consequently, no individual unit is willing to bear much of the cost, in time and effort, to produce the data that financial services consumes. Departments also see no advantage in timely production of billing data: If they produce and other departments do not, they gain nothing. The costs of data are correspondingly high to financial services, while the costs of information are low to the individual units in the hospital.

Furthermore, the exchange relationship is profoundly complicated by the complex structure — the hospital's dual authority (and dual value) system — since the departments that generate income and are the principal producers of input for billing and accounting view "efficiency" in terms of patient care rather than economics. In fact, the hospital's chief instruments of patient care delivery, the medical staff, can only with difficulty be held accountable for the hospital's financial health, and would be seen as stepping outside their value system if they exhibited excessive zeal for economic efficiency. It is frequently the opinion of medical units that the administrative staff exists to support their activities, not the other way around.

Another problem is time constraints upon the medical care staffs. Paperwork and record-keeping have to be performed in direct connection with patient care. Production of billing data can often be viewed as a function far enough removed from patient care to have a low priority. Data can ultimately be produced for billing purposes, but there is no guarantee that (1) they will be in the right form at the right time, or (2) other departments will go out of their way to produce them, since they see the production as essentially the responsibility of the administrative unit.

Structural complexity describes the general nature of exchange. Still other factors mediate the context of the exchange relationship, such as (1) interorganizational status competition, (2) the extent to which data production is a complicated process, (3) the number of levels between producer and consumer, and (4) the stability of agreements among exchange partners.

1. Interorganizational status competition enters into exchange in that whichever of two departments attempting to

negotiate an exchange is able to convince the other that it has higher status, can get the other to do more. The more capable a department is of convincing the other department of its higher status, the more deference it will have and the less it will pay for data.

2. The extent to which data production is a complicated process is a critical determinant of whether or not data are collected and reported. Simply stated, the more human effort is required to get the data out, the less likely it is that this will get done.

3. The number of levels between producer and consumer means that if data are not produced on time or are produced incorrectly and must be searched back, the more organizational levels there are to go through to reach the data source, the less likely the process will be successful.

4. The stability of agreements among producers and consumers relates to the extent to which everyone understands and agrees to the procedures of the production process. The more often the procedures have to be renegotiated because of change, the less likely the agreements will remain stable and in effect over time.

Before demonstrating the relationship of these four mediators to the production of data in the hospital, it is necessary to outline the hospital's billing process.

THE PROCESS

Financial services, among other things, produces the patient's bill. Before it can do so, it must get data from general intake facilities (admitting, emergency, and outpatient departments) that detail the financial obligations of patients and provide the appropriate information about their insurance, what happened to them in the hospital, and why. This requires data from professional departments, such as the laboratory or the pharmacy, that have performed services on behalf of the patient, as well as data from the therapeutic staff, which sees that not only treatment-related expenses such as syringes, special dressings, and drugs are included, but that all the miscellaneous items (soft drinks and food items) consumed by the patient are properly charged; otherwise they must be absorbed by the nursing unit itself. While these items are small individually, they add up to a significant amount over time and impact upon the unit's budget. Financial services must then get data from the medical records department, which functions as an intermediary between doctors in hospital departments and a number of external agencies. Medical records collects patient records, checks, then abstracts and collates statistics and other information. It then secures discharge diagnoses if they are missing, and files the completed record. Much of what this department does is mandated by law and consequently must conform to external criteria. Other practices are prescribed by professional ethics.

After patients are billed and the billing data have been compiled into the accounts receivable, financial services then prepares operating statements for each department summarizing the department's monthly activities in terms of income verses expenses along several indicators: personnel, fixed operating expenses, and variable expenses. The statement is supposed to depict budget activity to date, compare the activity with the previous month as well as with last year's performance, and give anticipated levels for the coming period. Most important, the statement is supposed to flag deviations and automatically report to the appropriate division manager where department performance is off standard. Finally, the information is stored for the next operating period as well as for the forthcoming budget year. The operating statement is designed to be an ongoing evaluation of each department, its productivity, and its management, and is the basis for negotiating the next year's budget. Departments need to receive these statements in order to self-correct when necessary or take advantages of profits to be gained if a systematic and timely analysis is followed.

For a number of reasons associated with getting the new reporting system to work, financial services was unable to produce operating statements on time, if at all, because it had to run the general ledger before it could do so, and that was delayed by errors in the accounts receivable and software problems. Over time, departments were disadvantaged because they had little control over their financial activities and found it difficult to tell if their actions were making things better or worse. When operating statements were issued three to four months late, contractual departments had major difficulties reporting to their parent company's auditors. Financial services was unable to output something others wanted in order to induce them to cooperate in producing the data financial services wanted. Departments began to feel that if they were not going to get what they needed, why cooperate at all?

1. The Role of Interorganizational Status Competition

Because status plays such a large role in exchange relations, it follows that each of those departments that are *close* in status positions will attempt to exploit any slack in the relationship to get the other to make the greater commitment to the exchange process. Greater commitment means that departments do more to produce data. The admitting department and financial services must work together closely, because admitting produces much of the insurance information which is basic to the billing process. The more complete the information is when it comes from admitting, the less time financial services will have to spend tracing down and completing the missing parts.

There is always a suspicion on the part of financial services that admitting has "lots more time," "more people," or really "goofs off a lot." Financial services claims that it is "up to Admitting to handle insurance material. . . . Our job begins when the insurance information is complete." Financial services sees the admitting department as a "roomful of clerks with more time than we have," which is not the way financial services refers to pharmacists or nurses, whose higher status, by virture of their patient care orientation, is not subject to negotiation.

Financial services always tries to get admitting to do more for financial services. This position was fostered early in the system study when the consultants recommended moving the admitting department into financial services on the basis of the similar functions and personnel. Financial services persisted, because the more financial services succeeded in defining admitting as a "similar" department, the more likely were its chances to pull admitting into its own complex, in a dependent position which, among other things, would assure financial services of a reliable supply of the necessary insurance data which it could control.

Admitting's defensive strategy was to refuse to acknowledge the definition financial services was seeking to impose on it — that is, of calling itself an administrative colleague. Instead, it opted to define itself as "definitely more related to patient care. . . . We are a direct link with the nursing units. It is nursing with whom we work most closely, not administration." By defining itself as a patient care department, it hoped to receive "protective coloration" to defend its boundaries against encroachments from financial services.

If the admitting department could succeed in getting itself defined as patient-care-related, then patient care values and priorities could enable it to produce billing data on its own terms: "We're here to help the patients. We try to get the most complete financial data we can, but we get busy and rushed and patients checking into a hospital are sick and anxious and often unable to cope with long questions and complex forms. The way we see it, getting financial data is mainly financial services' problem, not ours. Our biggest problem would be the wrong signature on a form, or, God help us, no signature at all. That might mean malpractice for the hospital. Believe me, that would be a problem." The way admitting sees it, they are giving as much to the exchange relationship as they are able to give, once their role in patient care is acknowledged. Admitting implies, furthermore, that financial services' preoccupation with financial data is out of place in the face of the daily drama in the admitting lounge, as borne out by the admitting supervisor, who said, "We are the first hospital department the patient has contact with. How he's treated in large part determines how he'll feel about the hospital. Furthermore, if financial services wants more complete data, it should be *here*. . . . They should try to get data out of old, collapsed patients or people scared out of their heads."

Financial services feels that "admitting should be more helpful. . . . Frankly, they are not as helpful as they could be. . . . They really should do a much better job of producing the documentation we need. For example, if they would verify the patient's insurance coverage, it would save us a lot of time and trouble." Financial services. feels it should be able to expect more from nonpatient care departments which resemble it in makeup. It feels it has no obligation to defer to status here.

A common complaint of producing departments is that consumers do not understand what goes on in producing departments or how much effort it takes to produce what is requested; data-processing and information systems "are mostly designed from the standpoint of the needs of one department or function at the expense of others." Characteristically, admitting felt that financial services showed little sympathy to its constraints or workloads, or that there were a number of circumstances in which it was just impossible to get complete insurance data." Admitting believed that system designers had failed to consider the priorities of producers equally with those of consumers.

In the transactions between these two departments, the designers of the system had failed to take into consideration the fact that each department had a greater stake in the operation of its own department than it did in the other's. The two departments were close in status. Absent from the exchange relationship was a status discrepancy that both partners could acknowledge as capable of defining the conditions of the exchange. Admitting tried to fabricate a discrepancy by claiming that it was in reality a patient care department and therefore was qualified to be treated like other patient care departments, that is, with deference. The financial services department, however, was not willing to acknowledge this definition, and went so far as to claim that admitting belonged within it because it performed essentially finance-related, not patient-care-related, functions.

Each department wanted the other one to do more of the job of getting and verifying insurance information. Each wanted to do less and to get or produce data cheaply. Each refused to accord the other one any degree of status or deference in the transaction. None of these problems had been anticipated when the system was designed.

2. Degree To Which Data Production Is Complicated

However, when the financial services department interacts with the short stay surgery department, it behaves differently, even though it is trying to get essentially the same kind of data it asks of admitting. Short stay's priorities are not oriented toward producing data for financial services, "unless there's enough time," for this section includes the emergency department as well as the six-hour surgery group. Financial services behaves differently because short stay is unambiguously a patient care department and one under time constraint, where all personnel, with the exception of clerks who have been specifically trained to process patients under stress, are medical practitioners. The department "is used to seeing patients where we have to get a maximum amount of information in a short time. . . . we are naturally interested in getting medical information or whatever relates to the emergency, and the patient may not be in a condition to tell us much, anyway." Circumstances might preclude "getting financial data, although clerks try and get what they can. We just can't hold long conversations, though."

The billing procedure for short stay differed from regular billing in that some patients were admitted to the hospital proper after emergency treatment and their accounts had to be merged into the regular accounts, while others left immediately after initial treatment. A standard method for sorting, billing, and transferring accounts was not worked out when the accounting system was first automated because accounting and data-processing personnel could not agree on one, so it was decided to handle the accounts from short stay on an ad hoc (manual) basis and see how the situation developed. Much sooner than anticipated, there was a sizable increase in these accounts. Hastily developed input forms were supplied to short stay to use for data transmittal, but forms were then amended, superseded, or discarded and replaced by other ones. The procedure was frequently changed and, overall, remained labor-intensive and complicated for short stay.

Short stay was not "terribly familiar" with the billing process, or why data had to meet deadlines. The unit really did not know how much it was losing on uncollectible accounts, but said that "even if it never made a dime, it would have its doors open 24 hours a day," because the unit was mandated. "The divisional manager comes down every now and then and shouts at us but we're used to it, and after all, we do *try* to get billing data. But to figure out which form is the right one or what changes have to be incorporated is a pain in the neck. Where are we supposed to get the time?" Furthermore, financial services "should come and get the data themselves."

Financial services has done just that on several occasions, for "such a backlog of incomplete records accumulates that we [financial services] send down two or three people to straighten out the mess and things are all right for a while." Even though financial services seems resigned to living with the situation and working hard to get its data, they face an ongoing struggle. At the recommendation of the consultants, financial services was advised to train short stay clerks and familiarize them with the billing problems so that they would be more sensitive and therefore more willing to get the data financial services needed. The grand idea was that financial services and short stay would "exchange and cross-train clerks for a couple of weeks." This would "promote close working relationships and a better understanding of how the personnel could help each other." Unfortunately, it was a "total fiasco": "The Short Stay clerks arrived when we were already under pressure with the new computer system. Right off the bat, they didn't like our offices.

They were too crowded. Theirs were better. Their desks were bigger. They missed the patients. They were bored. We were so glad to see them go — you can't believe the relief. . . . We were days straightening out the mess they'd managed to create in our offices." The financial services contingent did no better in short stay: "The first patient one of our billers encountered was bleeding rather freely and our biller promptly fainted. Another one had to get forms signed a few minutes before a woman gave birth. They didn't get their coffee breaks and their lunches were always late. They hated it and us!"

Did the job exchange promote better understanding of each other's work and data needs? Apparently not, since financial services was still working just as hard to get its data out of short stay almost a year later. Financial services was forced to accommodate a situation with first a status imbalance because of the patient care aspect. More important, financial services was indirectly responsible for initiating (by neglect) a difficult and tedious data transfer and collection process which required considerable time to complete. If that were not enough, financial services' brief tenure in the department caused it to experience firsthand the workload and the time constraints.

Nothing changes for short stay if they do not produce the data — there are no penalties, they would still be in business, and they know from experience that while they "may get yelled at," sooner or later, someone will come down and straighten out the records. In short stay's view, time is at such a premium that it is given to treatment and conforming to legal requirements; only if anything is left over can it then turn to the data needs of financial services. Short stay can do much less to produce what financial services wants, and can pass the costs of production on to financial services almost totally. It is likely that financial services will continue to pay high for the data it gets from short stay.

3. The Number of Levels between Producer and Consumer

Doctors are the generators of income. By bringing patients into the hospital, they initiate the chain of activities which brings money into the systems. But as a source of information about individual transactions on patient accounts, they are removed from the direct activities of financial services, because a number of levels, or human intermediaries, stand between doctors and financial services. The importance of a completed, fully documented medical record is an illustration of how control over data production is drastically weakened by the number of filters between producers and consumers.

From medical records, financial services needs to get a released patient record, for billing cannot begin until the patient has been officially discharged. An official discharge requires the patient's attending physician to complete the patient record with a summary discharge diagnosis, a date, and, above all, a signature. It is the responsibility of the medical records department to make sure this task is completed, and while it may seem simple and straightforward, it requires a mammoth effort; medical records is "almost permanently behind — it's only a matter of how far behind in our work we can stand to be."

It would be possible for the department to be more up to date if their entire operation could be computerized, but "since DP is so busy with financial services, we are waiting our turn. Only now with utilization review are we likely to be computerized. We must still wait for financial services to be functioning before we are brought onto the system." Medical records performs routine reporting functions on a number of statistical collections as well as special reports made at the request of the medical staff or another external agency. Some reports might be completed at the request of individual staff doctors or of management. The department must meet a number of deadlines for a number of reasons, in addition to monitoring records and verifying that records are complete.

A number of patient records are incomplete when they arrive. They may be missing a few data that are en route from another department, or waiting to be abstracted and collated. In any case, there are piles of records all over the office, and the staff complains that it is "permanently short-staffed" and that the effort has grown beyond its "present resources."

When financial services receives verification that a patient record has been signed off, it can queue that account for machine entry and collation of the other charges. Since medical records also sends verification to DP, the computer will automatically drop accounts into processing order. If the discharge diagnosis is not obtained, the account gets jammed and collection cannot be initiated on the bill. Furthermore, in certain cases the record itself must be made available to the fiscal intermediaries representing third-party payers; these intermediaries will regularly sample accounts, employing rigorous and complete analyses or researching the history of particular questions.

A major reason why records jam up and are incomplete is that doctors do not sign off the record. "Some doctors are always negligent, others are forgetful, busy or away. Some are reluctant to finalize the record, others are cautious, and a few hate paperwork and say so." The "permanent offenders often may have the most patients in the hospital. They resent being 'badgered' to sign off or they can't fit it into their schedule and find it easy to put off — it's like pulling teeth to get them in here." Since there is no substitute for the doctor's part in this task, the medical staff committee has provided procedures for reprimanding, censuring, and if necessary suspending errant doctors, but it would be highly unusual for a sanction to be applied, and in any case, if someone is a chronic offender, "even if he is corrected, he quickly relapses."

Since official sanctions do not work and since the hospital must get records signed off if it is to collect any of its money, what other methods exist to induce cooperation? "We telephone or write to the doctor's office, we find out when he's coming into the hospital, then go and wait for him on the floor or near the lunchroom. We have even waited outside the men's room!" If none of these strategies work, then medical records must "get hold of the assistant administrator and ask him to climb on the doctors' backs. He can do it better than I. I just can't go around nagging doctors. I have to work with them in so many ways that if I bugged them about records too, it might be the last straw and I'd never get any of the other things I need out of them."

The time between getting medical records and completing all their missing elements is long, but medical records feels "it can do little except wait." Financial services, however, considers "incomprehensible" the time records wait on data in the medical records department. Financial services finds it difficult to understand how records could "sit around," or that medical records cannot find a better way to deal with the backlog that in turn is delaying the billing process. Financial services complains that claims " worth thousands of dollars are regularly waiting around for doctors to sign off. . . . They are blocking cash flow into the hospital." At one point last year, more than $100,000 in claims [were] tied up pending discharge diagnoses.

Financial services feels that doctors "could be retrained to be more efficient since the government is placing greater and greater emphasis on medical justification for claim settlement. The doctors should be systematically trained to clear records more promptly." Who would be responsible for training the doctors? Financial services did not know, but did not think it was its job. Medical records and management both agree that only doctors can police doctors and that in any case, "It's a real drag to always be on someone's back over records." Financial services is concerned that months may pass before money is brought into the hospital once the billing process is started, so to delay it even more within the hospital is foolish.

Doctors are not moved by appeals to complete their records in order to bring money into the hospital. In any case, by bringing patients into the hospital in the first place, they believe that they make a contribution. Moreover, they know the hospital is in good financial health; otherwise they would not be associated with it. The doctors are concerned with ways to resolve their diagnostic uncertainty: There may be one more treatment or procedure they believe should be tried before the case is called closed.

Administrators do not "like to be the kind of person doctors avoid in the halls." As nonmedical supervisors of a medical component, they must depend upon their ability to strike reliable bargains on an ongoing basis. They may not wish to jeopardize their credibility too frequently with what could be interpreted as small and annoying problems, particularly if a doctor who generates a lot of income (brings a number of patients) for the hospital is involved.

Medical records neither wants to, nor can, coerce doctors into discharging records. To medical records, producing data for financial services is just one of many requests that it is adept at delaying. It does not mind seeing records pile up, for "there will always be more coming around, and if they're not missing signatures, they're missing something else." To medical records, the overload of paperwork is to be expected; it has "many other reports required by law or regulation which must be completed." It sees only a dim relationship between its records and the patient's bill, and is "not at all interested in the billing process." Medical records can gain nothing from speeding up its work to facilitate financial services, and believes it is "already doing all it can, particularly in view of the limitations on its own coercive powers."

While financial services waits on records, it can do little to hasten the process itself, for intermediaries separate it from the delinquent doctors. It can and does go to the assistant administrator to complain that records are "bogged down again," but this may not clear the bottleneck until the doctors actually find time to finish their part of the work.

Many reports work off the patient record, so even if the discharge diagnosis has been complete, the record may be "waiting on either a special report that has to go out this week, or being checked for the quarterly statistics, or held because a fiscal intermediary wants to know the average day's stay for certain types of patients." Therefore, standing between completed records and financial services are not just doctors at different levels, but other reports as well. All work off the same data on the one patient record. Everything stops or is held up if the record is incomplete. In any case, the result is to increase the distance between the hospital and its money.

4. The Stability of Agreements Over Time

Compiling a patient bill is a time-consuming process subject to numerous delays from the interplay of factors central to the exchanges between producers and consumers of data. Financial services' efforts can be eased if it can get departments to acknowledge deadlines for turning in billing data, and to conform to the procural requirements of the billing activity. Whenever departments fail to live up to the rules, however, financial services has to take time and effort to reestablish its requirements, adding further cost to its part in the data creation cycle.

Once financial services receives verification that the patient's record has been released for processing, it can begin to collate the numerous changes that constitute the patient's bill, feeding in charge data from other departments in the hospital. It is very important that bills go out complete, for months may elapse before actual payment is received from Medicare or Blue Cross. When providers receive additions or amendments after they have processed a bill for completion, it means they have to start all over again in the process. This is costly and more time is lost. Amended bills mailed to individual patients "are confusing and we must take time to explain them. More time is lost." If the hospital sends out a completed bill in one package, so to speak, it has a better chance of getting its money on time than it does if numerous additional bills go out on the same patient. The problem is how to do this.

Each department is supposed to generate its charges on time. Financial services complains that "many charges arrive after the bill has been mailed and necessitate a second billing. . . . We have told departments over and over. . . . Everyone said he understood and would cooperate, but when the next month rolled around, it was the same story all over. . . . Some people just don't get it through their heads that if we want to be paid, we have to have those charges to bill." In many cases, "people say that they understand, but they get caught up in something else and forget to process the billing data or the person who is supposed to do it is on vacation." It may even be that no one is really responsible for completing the billing data. "The lab, for example, which does several million dollars worth of business, does not have one designated person to see to it that charges are collected and sent down on a regular basis. Whoever isn't busy does it." Financial services added that it was "very difficult to get people to see the connection between money their departments generated and the translation of that income into operations, investments and so forth unless they're trained in administration."

THE PUBLIC VERSUS PRIVATE GOOD DILEMMA[1]

When departments produce data for other departments, those data have an opportunity cost in terms of what the department must forgo in order to do the work. Producing financial data is considered an inconvenience, a bother, even a "pain in the neck." Departments know that they must report money earned by the hospital in a timely and complete fashion or the hospital suffers, yet on an individual basis they do not see much to be gained whether or not they produce the data, because the process is troublesome, changeable, influenced by factors beyond their control, or provides no guarantee that the effort will result in a correct and timely operating statement. Central to a discussion of the costs of producing data are the notions of concentrated verses diffuse interests. *Concentrated interests* means that the effects of a policy, subsidy, or compulsion are significant to a given party. *Diffuse interests* is used to indicate unimportant benefits or costs to individual units, whatever the aggregate level of these costs or benefits is. Cast in terms of an organizational process model of politics, the incentives to press claims for concentrated interests are much greater than those for diffuse ones. The prospect of having one's well-being substantially affected creates incentives to protect one's interests. To have an interest that is marginal to one's well-being — even when the interest is aggregated over a large class and becomes enlarged — is still not to have substantial incentive to protect that interest.

In terms of the hospital, every unit would be better off providing data, but no one knows what others will do. No matter what units do, individual units are better off not providing data, for if a unit does provide it and others do not, it will get no information back from financial services, since the billing process is retarded until data are received from everyone; otherwise the costs of late data become overbearing. On the other hand, if the unit does not provide data and all the other units do provide, then the individual unit will benefit anyway, without the cost of producing. In this way, individually rational behavior results in collectively irrational behavior. Units perceive benefits as diffuse when they are not motivated to act. However, despite the fact that the costs to financial services are concentrated, merely having concentrated costs does not give it sufficient power for it to act politically to change the situation, particularly in light of the more powerful status resource the medical practitioners and their professional colleagues possess. A potential way to overcome the collective-good problem would be through a process that internalizes some of the rewards and externalizes some of the costs — that is, one that makes some of the good private instead of collective. For example, units that do not contribute their data might be penalized with a service charge or the deduction of productivity points. Those which do comply in a timely and accurate way can be rewarded.

Department managers had no incentives to produce. A frequent complaint of managers was that they "did not see the results of their work." The charge reports were not returned in the form of operating statements or budget analyses items important to department managers and valuable to their work. In fact, operating statements were backlogged three or four months, because financial services had so much trouble in subunits of the system that integration of data could not be managed without high risk of error. The lack of statements was causing a strain on departments because they could not relate expense and income figures in order to know how they stood. They did not know if they were over-budget, were under-budget, could spend money, could hire help, could invest in new equipment, or should retrench. They expressed fears that they would find out too late.

The inability of financial services to produce operating statements and budget summaries deprived financial services of negotiating capital and added to the tensions within the process. Moreover, there had already been several confrontations between various departments and the head of financial services. But the problems remained unresolved. Financial services was involved with getting the information system to work and "simply could not get sensible output from the computer." Most departments were aware that they were coming off poorly in the exchange process: "They [financial services] lay all these demands on us to get their stuff to them, but when it comes to getting what we need, you'd think we were asking for state secrets by asking for a lousy operating statement that even rinky-dink organizations produce like clockwork."

Characteristically, departments failed to see that they were contributing to the delays in the process, or that one problem triggered another. When financial services responded that they were "having problems getting the new system into operation," departments were scarcely sympathetic: "They're in a mess over there. . . . Frankly, they've been having problems far too long."

A disadvantage in large, complex organizations is that individuals are separated from the results of their work. They do not see the connection between the money they generate for the organization through their services and the eventual translation of that money into operations and investments, unless they are not directly concerned with accounting. Similarly, they fail to realize that delays originating with them carry over to other departments and are costly and inconvenient.

In terms of the departments that were supposed to generate input for the billing cycle, an additonal set of structural variations impacted on the data production process. None of these variations has been anticipated in planning the system requirements:

(1) Time delays were often due to variations in department work schedules: "Our workload is variable. There are days that are so busy that we don't have time for anything else but the most pressing professional or patient-related paperwork. When things quiet down, then we have to catch up on our own overdue paperwork before we can think about doing work for other departments."

(2) Variable outputs also result from a variable workload: "Some days we don't have enough charges to merit the cost of making up the report. We'd rather save them up until we have enough, since it takes as much work to fill out forms for a few as it does for a lot."

(3) Charges were incomplete because they were waiting on additional work: "Sometimes the results of one test will call forth additional ones, or maybe we will get a report back that we should rerun a procedure. It's more complicated to catch and amend a charge than it is to wait until it's complete."

(4) Charge data were not available, or there were price changes: "We have to set aside time to verify charges and check for increases and decreases as well as differences due to substitutions of brands or products."

(5) Forms are not readily available for recording charges: "If we run out, we have to wait until someone remembers and goes down to the first floor and brings them back."

More problems resulted from professionals who headed departments and were either too busy or found paperwork too distasteful to do the charge work themselves. If they did not have an administrative assistant, they were relunctant "to lay it on a colleague who doesn't like it any more than I do." Professionals became preoccupied with the substantive content of their work and forgot about or were disinterested in supervising the work of clerks whose job it was to produce the data. As medical technology put it, it was "the 'Chief Tech's' job to supervise the paperwork, but once he gets his eyeball clamped to the microscope, he's dead to the world." Since good professionals are scarce, the department is hardly likely to want to waste its efforts training them to do paperwork for other departments. Besides, they "really don't have time for extra paperwork. Look, if charges don't get sent down, and financial services loses a deadline, all they lose is time, and they get paid anyway. If we neglect our work to do theirs, then we're liable to goof up and jeopardize someone's life. If our medical recording is not absolutely correct, we could lose our accreditation."

WHY FINANCIAL SERVICES CONSUMES EXPENSIVE DATA

In the absence of a price mechanism, one way of viewing the cost of data is to consider it a function of the extent of effort that must be expended to get the data. Financial services expends considerable energy, in the form of special efforts, various persuasive strategies, merely waiting on other departments to produce, or bearing their resentment and lack of cooperation.

WHEN ARE DATA EXPENSIVE?

From the standpoint of financial services, data became expensive, first, because they came off badly in the struggle for status capable of coercing deference, and second, because there was no generally agreed upon contract between it and other departments about who should do what. Each department tried to make a savings in time and effort by having financial services make the disproportionate share to the commitment.

Data were expensive because procedures were unclear, complicated, and time-consuming, or because forms were un-

TABLE 1 Getting Data

Exchange Partner	Status in re FS	FS Wants	FS Can Offer	Does It?	FS Gets Data?	How?	Way It Wants?
Admitting	=	Insurance data	Deference	No	Often incomplete	Threat complaint	No
Emergency	+	Insurance data	Better forms	No	Usually incomplete	Does it itself	No
Doctors	+	Discharged records	—	—	Very late	Administrative coercion	No
Other departments	+	Charges	Forms budget data instruction	No	Late; incomplete	Administrative coercion; persuasion helps do it	No

standardized, uncoded, and difficult to locate. Complicated charge reporting was assigned to a special person in a department when there was no one else to do the work, because departments could not afford to consume time to teach the process to others.

Data were expensive when there was no recourse to the producer because a number of intermediaries separated producer and consumer. When it was impossible to go directly to the doctors and explain why their completed records were needed, financial services had to wait around on work until higher authorities had the time and attention to get to the doctors.

Finally, data were expensive because financial services and the departments failed to negotiate stable contracts to conduct business. The departments expected to get something in return for their efforts. They expected a tangible return, such as operating statements (reports vital to their work), or a social benefit, such as understanding or appreciation. In most cases, however, when the payoff was too vague or too far in the future, it was unlikely to be of sufficient interest to producers to motivate them to maintain a contract. The price of data increases sharply when agreements over transactions must constantly be negotiated and renegotiated.

One of the goals financial services hoped to achieve with its MIS was higher status, to impove its bargaining position in the organization. Often, computers, through their imposition upon the organization of a structured world view, can add to a department's authority to make demands in the name of rationality or order, which may offset whatever imbalance in status relations exists.

Financial services pays a high price for the data it needs. Is it a fair price? In a normal market, one that deals with goods and services, suppliers set prices equal to their marginal costs. Yet we cannot apply this analogy to the hospital billing system, for departments know that bills will get out anyway. Thus it is in their best interest to expend as little effort as possible and to keep their marginal costs low. Clearly, it is in the interests of departments to be free riders, since financial services is, so to speak, stuck with providing the public good. Only if the cost of providing data is defined as an externality instead of a public good will there be a need for producers to produce their own data. This means that producers will have to assume some of the costs of data production or else compensate financial services, in the form of a service payment, for doing it for them.

In terms of the MIS, when departments have different values and priority structures and are judged by different measures of achievement, they must perceive some gain to be made by putting aside their own priorities in order to produce data for other departments. If departments or units do not see that they will get anything in return or if the reward is far in the future, they are understandably reluctant to go out of their way to produce data, which costs them time and effort and nets them little in return.

NOTE

1. See Olson, 1971.

Processing Complexity

THE PURPOSES OF INFORMATION SYS-
TEMS, generally speaking, vary according to their location in
the spectrum of decision. Some systems merely tabulate and
summarize daily events on a regular, ongoing basis, and deliver
"state" reports: This is where we stand as of the end of the
quarter. Other systems monitor ongoing activities in order to
locate and report when the unexpected has occurred. Others
are, in the words of Simon and associates(1954), scorecard
systems designed to address the meaning of different sets of
data: Are things worse or better if this trend continues? Still
others perform problem identification functions to denote
where action is needed or to direct attention to issues requiring
deeper consideration.

Realistically speaking, an information system designed to
address the entire decision spectrum, from problem identification to analysis of alternative strategies and choice of action,
would need to have the capability of not only processing transactions and generating routine reports, but the ability to be
model-based as well. A model-based system is mathematically
described. The system, using carefully defined parameters, can
manipulate data within a theory in order to produce information

69

to forecast, simulate, or optimize an organization's activities. Such systems are usually referred to as "total" systems, and demand, among other things, wholesale changes in outlook and procedures, expensive hardware and software, large data bases and a competent professional staff.

THE TOTAL INFORMATION SYSTEM IDEA

A total hospital information system would integrate the medical components with the administrative ones to free the time of professionals, relieve the paperwork burden, provide more accurate diagnoses and implementation of doctors' orders, improve the quality of patient-care-planning, and define strategies for reducing the costs of medical care. At present, the total hospital information system is more an ideal than a reality. Sooner or later, most hospitals are able to get the traditional business functions under some control, but not all hospitals are even able to bring about improvements in financial information — that is, better information on a timely basis and at a lower cost — let alone move to the total information concept. Frequently, many data, rather than better information, are produced. Some of the problems associated with improving financial information are noteworthy if one wishes to understand why computer-based systems fail to have any major impact on the cost of caring for patients.

Essential to the total hospital information system idea is that computer applications integrate into one system with a shared data base, and that ongoing monitoring provide relevant feedback as soon as any deviations from a prescribed optimum are detected. The collection and recording of data is a central issue in a total system, as well as in any integrated system, because in order for the computer to access the data base accurately and provide input into decision-making, the "rules of transformation" and standards of performance must be rigidly predefined and specified for each decision. Too often the extreme narrowness of this approach inhibits effective operation, in that available data simply will not fit the requirements of the computer program or the information base. One response is to expand the base and add still another class of rigidly defined and equally narrow instances to cover the current contingency.

TYPICAL DESIGN APPROACHES

Caught between so many sets of conflicting demands, information systems designers frequently find themselves forced to take one of two approaches. The first is the pool approach: Collect everything that might be useful to potential users; construct large data banks with coding, updating, and indexing, and perhaps an infinite pool of data will be created and managers will pull out whatever they need. The second approach is to attempt to scrap the general collectivity and opt for *management by exception* (Ackoff, 1967). Here the idea is to filter out those data which are not supposed to change the decision maker's view of nature, and have the system do the searching and filtering by determining when a given type of data should be provided.

THE POOL APPROACH

The problem with the pool approach is that a large, comprehensive data base results in an overabundance of data. If a manager wants to use these data, he or she must spend time searching, collating, and condensing a quantity of data. If the manager does not use the data but still needs data, then an alternative source must be found. In both instances, the costs of filtering data for decision-making are transferred to the user, either in time and resources to filter what the user gets, or in time and resources to get elsewhere what is not obtained from the system. There is, of course, no guarantee that either data will be relevant or error-free.

There are several reasons that designers cannot give managers relevant data:

1. Users cannot describe their needs in sufficient detail. Much of the service to users at the billing level was oriented toward billing, based on both standard operating procedures for billing and billers' descriptions of their own work. Months into the system, "DP was still attempting to add upwards of 200 details that had been overlooked in job descriptions, but without which the system didn't make sense."

2. Users may not know in advance what their requirements will be, particularly if changes in needs are predicated upon changes of other users, or upon what one report says. These changes may be prompted or imposed from outside and may change quickly and unexpectedly. Government format requirements for billing reports "were changing so fast that we no sooner got one set into the system when another circular came out requiring more changes, or even cancelling what the last report had decreed."

3. Understanding may be possible only on a case-by-case basis. This knowledge may be slow, expensive, and limited in its application, but it is the only means of building a data base. For example, "since the geriatrics department is new and we're not even sure yet what it encompasses, we can't even begin to make use of the computer." This may make "the cost of a human information system certainly much less, when you consider quality and speed of report."

The system would still have to be informed by some measure of utility. Getting a faster response time may be a pointless expense if the report is still in error or unusable in its format, or sits on a user's desk.

The pool approach is expensive because it consumes resources to construct a data bank that is in a continuing state of expansion and requires storage and updating, but still frustrates its users and does not answer their questions. Users cannot learn enough of what works because the number of variables is great. Furthermore, the less something is understood, the more data will be needed to explain it.

THE EXCEPTION APPROACH

The exception approach to the problem of providing users with relevant information is one which lets the system decide, by means of a performance standard, when a given type of data should be provided. The costs of filtering are borne by the system. This approach places responsibility upon managers to describe their task environments accurately, and upon system designers to interpret accurately the relevant variables and relationships. The exception approach treats the organization as a closed system, where the validity of the standard is a function of the number of interrelationships that must be calculated to arrive at the standard. The more there are, the less coherent the standard is likely to be. Another approach removes all constants from a computer program and reads them in as parameters at execution time. Most exception-type systems are not particularly sensitive to individual or "just noticeable differences" (Tversky and Kahneman, 1974).

However, even if the model were to report exceptions rather than constants, it would eventually end up becoming just as rigid and inflexible as the constant model, in that the number of "essential" and "conditional" exceptions for every set of users in a hospital is flexible and would be quite staggering in a general-purpose model. The larger and more general the system attempts to be, the greater are its requirements and data entry procedures. It is then likely to cause departments to come into conflict over what should be the purpose of the system as well as whose view of reality should obtain.

There are a number of reasons designers are unable to give managers the data they consider relevant:

1. The system needs the capability to recognize exception-type cases for all users under all circumstances. Yet exceptions are pronounced in the system. Even billers might give one set of terms to one client and another set to another client for the same services, if there was a greater possibility of collecting more of the money owed to the hospital. At a higher organiza-

tional level, there is a need to track and rapidly analyze the revenue produced by cost centers for each type of procedure. At still another level, changes in room expenses such as housekeeping, food, nursing, heat, and power, are to be continuously analyzed to reflect increases or decreases requiring recalculation of expenses, and changes in hospital's finances.

2. The exception system needs to know what action to take under all circumstances, a capability that is either impossible or too expensive. This would have to include exceptions at all levels to detail, including the level where exceptions predominate: organizational leadership.

Since system requisites are so stringent, the system usually ends up displaying anything that remotely resembles an exception. This increases both the cost and the quantity of output. The user has to scan vast reports and still may not catch all necessary exceptions. Balance forward procedures routinely registered exception cases according to the account's age. If a biller coded an accoumt as "under special treatment," after a set period of days had passed, no matter what the circumstances, the computer automatically rejected the special treatment code and recorded the account in the "process for collection" category. To cancel this operation required complicated human intervention into the system.

4. If the system does not select, the user must, and users vary greatly in their definition of exceptions at their level of the organization. Furthermore, parametric changes are so variable that the system often automatically selects a default option before the user has a chance to choose.

5. The system cannot cope with continual change, or does so at the expense of other features. Reducing the response time of the sequential processing of the data base required considerably reducing the batch cycle. Processing small batches was inefficient, however, since this increased the "bitty-ness" of reports, led to piles of paper, generally confused everyone, and inevitably increased error. Yet, if the data base were to be rather quickly updated, it could only be done in this fashion, to conform to system specifications.

6. Increasing selectivity makes the system expensive, since many users make for many demands. The more the volume of expensive data grows, the more system maintenance increases in cost. Adminstrative overhead may become prohibitive, or the system gets so complicated mechanically that it is burdensome. Attempts to develop sophisticated reporting systems for the hospital necessitated bringing in special expertise from outside in the form of engineering, rather than analytic, support. Unfortunately, the "expensive engineers developed expensive, complicated systems that only engineeres, not managers, could understand." In addition, as the data base grows, storage and retrieval costs also grow, and response time slows.

7. Finally, aside from technical costs, exception reporting systems have political costs in terms of the ability to understand the activities of any user, as well as in terms of a retreat from the principles of general system theory. Managers, particularly health care professionals, may feel that the power of exception-type problems lies in their dependence on the judgment and ability of the managers, not on the system. To give up this option may mean revealing skills or factors that could expose decision makers to risk from other elements of the organization, or give away data they are not willing or able to disclose. Attempts to introduce exception systems may be viewed either as attempts to cut off options or decrease decision makers' influence by decreasing their access to information about organizational goings-on, or as a way of familiarizing decision makers with what might be useful at some later time.

Attempts to introduce exception power can also be viewed as retreats from a commitment to a general information system. These attempts often increase organizational conflict because users may have to justify, compromise, or otherwise petition competitively for time on the system, bargaining over options. There is more stress among users when they see others getting options they believe may have been denied to them.

The exception-type system assumes a commonality of interests that is unrealistic, since inappropriate criteria will not encompass the multifaceted nature of the organization. A tradeoff between quantity and quality, if made by the data-processing department, may lead to a deterioration in quality and an increase in the cost-effective (for them) quantity of data processed. If the same tradeoff is made by users, then quantity may be sacrificed, and data-processing is asked to bear the costs of special exception quality.

IMPACT OF COMPLEXITY

Utilization review and PSRO regulations have also added to the complexity as well as the size of the data base. Regulations on Medicare/Medicaid accounts provide that on admission patients are to be assigned a length of stay which is age and diagnosis-specific. The physician's plan of care and a statement of whether or not the patient needs to be in the hospital must be included. An investigation must be conducted to determine that the patient is receiving the appropriate medical care for the diagnosis. Retrospective audits are also to be conducted on physicians whose patterns of care or diagnoses lead to excessive cost.

A number of steps are required to meet these utilization/ PSRO regulations:[1]

(1) diagnosis and assignment of length of stay;

(2) daily examination of the chart to ensure the physician has started treatment;

(3) a file set up for the length of stay so the patient's record can be examined on that day;

(4) daily removal of discharged patients;

(5) daily review of the medical record by a competent person to see what has been done for the patient in relation to what should have been done;

(6) extension of the patient's stay if medically necessary, after obtaining the required verifications;

(7) appropriate notation made for Medicare/Medicaid billing; and

(8) reporting of diagnostic information to the intermediary and the PSRO group.

The process requires close cooperation between data-processing, medical records, and medical and financial service departments, because the charges collected by the business office must be translated into a profile of the medical care going on in the hospital. The patient record is the central communication link between all departments in the health care facility.

THE PATIENT RECORD

The medical records system also provides sets of monthly and yearly reports to administration for the purpose of assessing the facility's major activities. These reports include summaries of medical and business services with clinical patterns of practice, death and discharge listings, tissue, infections, and gynecology reports, and incipient diagnostic. The information contained in these reports is derived from the patient records. Therefore, it is important to consider the problems that may be associated with this primary source of communication in order to assess their impact on accurate translation of the patient record into both daily and major reports.

1. The record does not include all the relevant information: Much information is translated verbally. Nursing shifts have reports where patient care information and gossip are transmitted from the offgoing to the oncoming shift. Physicians gather in the halls for informal consultation or to check with health care personnel for updates on patients that may never appear in the written documents in as great detail, particularly if the patient is a V.I.P. This communication contributes to patient care but essentially bypasses formal documentation.

2. Medical terminology presents a barrier. Health care personnel vary in education levels. Often an insurance clerk fills

out the diagnosis and the operative procedures. Often the clerk
is not medically trained and lists an inaccurate diagnosis. The
medical terminology may be interpreted incorrectly or arbitrarily. Chest pains could represent myocardial infarction or indi-
gestion. The wrong coding impacts on length-of-stay figures
and the wrong tabulation can ultimately grossly distort the
hospital's pattern of care. Medical departments can function
around such error possiblities by using verbal communication.

3. Handwriting may be impossible to read. Some entries
are easier to read than others. Under time pressures, the legible
gets read, while the illegible may be set aside for further
questions or even guessed at. Phrasing can hinder or distort
interpretative frames of reference, with consequences for data
interpretation.

4. There are intermediate levels between the source of data
(the patient) and the eventual recording in the patient chart.
The aide spends the most amount of time face-to-face with the
patient but does the least recording. The aide communicates
verbally with the nurse, who communicates with the physician,
who writes the greatest amount into the record.

5. Fiscal reporting stringencies may make it necessary to
phrase a diagnosis in a particular manner that does not exactly
suit the patient's condition, in order to ensure payment. A
diagnosis may be tentative. Since billing figures are diagnosis-
related, these figures could be significantly distorted in the
end-of-the-month review.

6. The publicness of the record may dictate caution. The
record may be read aloud in court, read by the patient himself,
reviewed by in-house committees for PSRO purposes, and
abstracted and sent to external fiscal and governmental
authorities. All this not only suggests simple human prudence,
but that complete documentation could be counter to self-
interest.

Documentation is vital not only as the communication link
between professionals who never see each other but treat the
same patient, but also for legal, financial, and evaluative purposes and interfaces. The patient record formally ties the entire
system together, but, because of the very constraints of indi-

vidual purpose and objective, does not in fact include all the information "relevant" to a management information system.

PROBLEMS OF LINKAGES

The hospital is hooked together through the patient record, whereby many reports compiled by data-processing become a data base composed of as many data banks as there are systems in the hospital. The patient records are the main artery of transmission. The record is acted upon serially by the various departments, and becomes the integrative mechanism that enables the hospital to effect service delivery. The individual record provides the decision premises for treating the patient. Aggregates of patient records provide the reports that physicians and administrators and agencies consider vital for an accurate assessment of their major activities. The record is, in truth, the "conceptual focus" that Anand (1971) saw motivating the hospital.

The linking together of units for the purposes of completing billing, controlling, reporting, and evaluating performance is one of interdependence. The departmental organization of the hospital, however, is one emphasizing extreme independence with only weak links to other departments. No department is willing to give up its autonomy, nor do inducements within the system exist to encourage departments to do so. Rarely can scheduling activities — say between admitting, operating, and radiology — be coordinated. Departments must wait on data, delaying their recording on the patient record and in turn delaying other departments.

PROBLEMS OF MULTIPURPOSE SYSTEMS

Multipurposefulness tries to substitute for theory which does not exist and for cooperation which cannot be induced.

Using either an exception or a general pool approach, it outputs standards and logical rules of behavior. Due to the absence of clear understandings about what is information and what purpose it serves, system designers end up making a large system. Often responsibility for problems of coordination is transferred to the system itself, reflected in narrow data entry procedures, rigid programs, and tight time frames. As users change to adapt to constraints within their operational environment and within the information system itself, adaptions further increase the size and complexity of the system as well as the costs of coordination. The system becomes "expensive," "slow," ill-suited to anyone's needs, and plainly overlarge. Some reasons for the general dissatisfaction follow.

1. Each department consumes reports as well as produces reports. At the operations level, billing and insurance data are consumed; bills, statements, and reports to carriers and the general ledger are produced. Participants at different levels may or may not interact. The fiscal intermediary representing Medicare may or may not interact with the biller producing the data he or she will consume. "She usually . . . talks with the department manager or the assistant or hunts down records for herself." If "not satisfied with a reconstruction based on the patient record, she may request an explanation or a particular point from a department. . . . The department manager will then ask the assistant manager to 'look into it' with the department involved." If the problem involves a doctor, "she might tell the manager, who will talk with the administrator, and he in turn will delegate the problem to the assistant administrator in charge of professional services, who will get ahold of the doctor." The consumer of particular data has no [access] to the producer, except in rare instances, and is also separated by intermediaries who are external to the original transaction.

2. In every department there is a large proportion of exception cases. The considerable decentralization within the organization specifies outcomes but does not prescribe the "one best way" to achieve the desired outcome. For example, the hospital is interested in receiving as much of the money owed to

it as it can, so it may "offer one kind of credit terms to one private patient, another kind to different patients, depending on circumstances and the discretion of the biller in charge of the account." Standardization in coverage exists for Medicare/ Medicaid patients, but treatment may vary by physician. An insurance carrier may cover all of a particular procedure, while another covers a differential amount of the same procedure. Medicare may pay one patient's claim "for the same treatment it questions in another patient," or one doctor may order one kind of treatment for a patient with a particular complaint, while another doctor orders a different treatment for another patient with the same complaint.

3. Each department needs data it can manipulate: Billers must distribute charges into billing parameters of carriers until the most advantageous fit is achieved. At the managerial level, pricing structures must be manipulated and shortfalls from retrospective payment identified or consideration given to the meaning of, say, a 15 percent increase in the amount of Medicare patients. At the organizational level, there is a concern with methods for relating costs and benefits in such a way that services that are losers do not obliterate gainers, so that charges and costs can be determined rationally.

4. There are contradictory demands in purposes. The hospital may want to look good to its investors, who want to know their money is being used properly, yet it may not want to look all that good to authorities, who hold veto power over its plans. When our hospital applied to authorities for an extension of its eastern boundary, it was informally told that "the application would probably be denied: We're doing well financially and another hospital has been tacitly promised it could extend into this [upper-middle-class] area. We would have no difficulty extending southward, but then we'd pick up a large percentage of Medicaid and Medicare patients, which we can't afford to do." If "we appear to the government to be managing well, then we risk having the squeeze put on us, and our services and delivery priced too low."

The hospital's information system used a model that was supposed to respond to a number of different departments, some of which needed very precise, detailed, individualized, current data, and some of which needed information focused against different indicators over substantial swatches of time, with broad pictures of what could be expected. Different departments in turn had different clients with different objectives and who wished to influence data they received. In addition to the general groupings of operations, managerial, and institutional level decision makers, there were other information consumers between levels who worked on specific tasks. Their aims could also be in conflict with those of the users at levels above and below them.

DID CONSUMERS GET THE REPORTS THEY NEEDED?

We get a better idea if we look at these reports from the standpoint of user levels within financial services itself.

1. Billers

Billers are supposed to manage their accounts in an efficient manner, which means that accounts are being pursued in such a way that the level of gains rises and the level of losses decreases. To accomplish this, a biller will have to be "conscientious about seeing that all patient charges are included, supervising the correct billing, following up on unpaid accounts, settling disputes quickly, and in general, handling the accounts so that they produce income."

To handle accounts efficiently, billers need daily reports capable of reflecting the status of each account, summarizing all activity on each account, and displaying the data simply, clearly, accurately, and promptly. There should be a control subsystem which reflects changes and corrections in the master system. All should be readily and easily accessed. The billers would then produce reports on a weekly basis reflecting the productivity of their work in terms of numbers and dollar values of accounts in various stages of processing, not yet processed, or in queue or backlog. Billers would have to enter details of disputes and to account for money owed to the hospital so that it would be possible to know the content (private coverage, government, prepaid) as well as when money is anticipated.

Much of the billers' daily work involves rapid assessment: "A patient calls and asks for an explanation of his bill, or a carrier might want to know why patient X was here for ten days and patient Y for seven days with the same illness." Consequently, billers need a way of getting this information from reports produced in the system rather than from original documents (e.g., patient records), which are generally inaccessible.

First, reports did not bear significantly upon the actual activities of billers, since each biller structured her activities according to her own account domain and prioritizing of what needed to be done. One person could be arbitrating an insurance dispute, another preparing accounts for Medicare logging, which required one type of listing process, while another could be doing privately paid accounts, which required a different kind of listing. The computer was unable to accommodate procedural variety and treated accounts alike. Where Medicare "required strict adherence in terms of coding and format, the computer transferred coding sets to private paid accounts where they were unintelligible, so the next day . . . there would be telephone inquiries about bills."

Second, reports were not of sufficiently recent vintage. The large model required early closing dates; hence "the report was old or out of balance by the time it arrived because it didn't include recent activity on accounts, as were the statements mailed at the same time, so people would call up and ask for an explanation." Accounts could not be billed until charges were received from all the departments. "At least in theory that was true. What actually happened was that departments would produce amended or additional charges after their first submission, or charges would dribble in after the cycle closed. The computer wasn't able to incorporate additions once the run began, so the extra charges had to be billed separately or else saved for the next cycle. . . . Typically, a patient would be mailed a bill. Two or three days later, we would send him an addendum of charges we had not included, then a few days later, another bill with more charges we had left out — all supplements of his original bill. He would generally hit the ceiling and call us on the phone asking where it would end. A bill might have three and four tag-ons mailed like oversights." Major carriers "were particularly hard-hit by this system of installment billing because it cost them money to receive bills after they'd started their process, and they'd have to pull the account out and reformat."

Reports reflected badly on the billers in that they "could not assess their own productivity." "There were no indicators for time spent running down charges on an account. . . . Accounts could be in abeyance merely because they were waiting on charges, but they would be logged by the computer as disputed or stalled in problem categories . . . making it look like billers had enormous amounts of disputed accounts and problems on their hands, when the only dispute was getting people to produce their input." Billers resented "having a low productivity rating when the actual fault lay with other people."

Reports were improperly formatted for billers. The most useful report was the account status report listed by alphabetical classification. This enabled billers to trace inquiries on accounts more easily, for "when patients called, they referred to their accounts by their names, rather than account numbers, and since numbers were long, it was easier to call a department and discuss an account by patient name. Names were also needed as verification if it was necessary to get data off a chart or make corrections for inputting." However, the "alpha listing was printed only after the account analysis report was completed." The analysis report was useful to management for making up the position reports, and to data-processing, for it enabled the computer to balance quicker, "but hours or days might elapse [before] the alpha list was produced from it." In order to use the numerical report, billers needed "to get the patient's name, go across the room to a file and look up the corresponding number, then go and find the account analysis and compare, all of which was time-consuming and left possibilities for errors." In a similar function, other reports were formatted so that they suited one function's purposes, but not those of another, which got the same report. People might get a number of printouts of different reports tabulating data across indicators, only one or two of which they could actually use, some of which they "couldn't even understand." They would combine the printouts into their own version by "cutting, folding, Scotch-taping together — the old Mickey Mouse method — until they got what they needed."

Throughout the installation, billers complained that "of all the people put out by the new system," they suffered the most inconvenience. Their output fell below what it had been under the old system, while their numbers were expanded to cope with the output of the new one. They claimed that they derived very little benefit from working with the new system, and that, in fact, much time was lost in getting it to produce what was needed.

2. Operations Supervisor

The operations level is supposed to bridge the gap between daily operations and management. It is concerned with the fitting together of personnel and tasks according to plans made at the executive level. On one hand, it filters data by suppressing detail; on the other, it is supposed to drive information upward by relating tasks and personnel in terms of productivity. In financial services, the supervisor, by virtue of her dual function as data control supervisor, was concerned with pricing and charge collections, "all problems associated with our end of the computer," and the development of work procedures, personnel, and productivity as well. The supervisor's work involves the fulfillment of preestablished targets for productivity, time-scheduling, work assignments, evaluation of workloads, performances, and training. She reports on these indicators to the department manager. In addition, she does liaison work with insurance carriers and various intermediaries, makes reports on pricing and cost prediction, and provides accounting support for a number of reports (e.g., profit and loss, credit, changes in cash position).

The main bulk of the supervisor's work, once the computer was functioning, was related, however, "to the error problem, to straightening out one error after another," as well as "training people over and over to work with the computer and to understand the problems it and they made." Supervisors need reports sensitive to impressionistic analysis. Reports that "highlighted exceptional cases would be useful to help determine alternative courses of action, such as whether or not there was a cheaper way of handling certain accounts." There would be a need for a "weekly summary of account activity reflecting the general condition of the hospital's accounts receivable," as well as a "productivity summary that could show trends and could be used as a control mechanism capable of determining levels, showing where new personnel were needed, testing the effects of training, and, in general, serving as a guide to the cost of operations.

WERE REPORTS USEFUL?

As an aid to decision, reports consumed by the supervisor and her assistants "were not helpful." The primary problem was that the more the system deviated from its expected course, the more the supervisor's actual work changed to meet the demands of the deviations. It was then difficult, if not impossible, to anticipate what information would be needed at what point in the work process. The supervisor's job was "related to whatever crisis was happening at the moment." Deviations "broke the programming in the billing process, and under the pressure of time and overlap, had to be resolved by essentially ad hoc methods." The workload "could be better described as general crisis, the resolution of pressing problems, interspersed with brief and unexpected and suspicious normalcy." Supervisors had little control over problem definition because "it was difficult to tell when a routine had been established and when we were operating in a crisis state." This situation was "a direct outcome of the billers' inability to resolve problems in the data base."

Problems were compounded by the necessity at least partly to retain the old system in order to get work produced, and as a guide to current operations. The "more errors occurred in the new system, the more it was necessary to revert to the old." Consequently, billers experienced reluctance to "learn new methods when it appeared that these methods might not work out, or might be supplanted, and they would have to use the old ones after all." In addition, the "more insecure people became, the more unwilling they were to trust the computer output." For example, "we would find people using their desk calculators to check and verify output. When we showed them that it was unnecessary and time-consuming to do that, that they should take the printout as a 'given,' so to speak, they wouldn't believe us, or right at that point a massive boner would appear in a printout. We took away all the desk calculators in order to force them to use the computer system. . . . they showed up with pocket calculators."

Unevenness and error in output caused serious morale problems. The conversion to the new system incredibly coincided with the department's remodeling program, and there was a high noise level as well as chaos and inconvenience caused by carpenters and painters working in the office. The error in timing "sent tempers escalating and increased stress." Ordinarily, "angelic people had tantrums, got hysterical over errors they uncovered, or interpreted the lack of cooperation from other departments as personal vendettas." Endless comparisons of workloads "were ongoing activities, and when one person discovered another apparently doing less work, complaints would result." Tension got so bad that people "really freaked out over production problems, and one assistant had a nervous collapse." In general, absenteeism and requests for transfers increased. Others "feared that their jobs would be eliminated or changed into something they couldn't cope with." The result for the supervision of operations was that much time had to be devoted to resolving (1) system problems, and (2) the effects of system problems on human users. The work of supervision was increased: "It became much more difficult and incredibly time-consuming."

The length of turnabout time meant that reports the supervisors received from the system seldom tabulated with reports received from the department. In many cases, reports were produced "days after scheduling and hiring problems had been resolved and could only be useful retrospectively, or as ex post facto justification." In other cases they indicated problems supervisors had long ago attended to. In most cases, the best way to find out what was actually going on was not to read the reports, but "to go around and ask the billers how they were doing."

An insurmountable problem was that operations supervision required reports that were cumulative in order to trace errors, as well as comprehensive in order to understand the effect of errors (Is it in category A or B, and what does it mean?). The system produced the same reports it produced at the billing level, but where billers received daily reports, operations got daily, weekly, and monthly accumulations. Reports were "either summary or comprehensive, *but not both.*" To make a useful report, the supervisor or one of the assistants had to "paw through the reams of bulky data in order to extract the appropriate sets for compiling a management report. Since no one had time or inclination," the reports accumulated until "we had no choice but to deal with them because we'd reached a point where we couldn't go on."

Reports were inaccurate. Because they were old by the time supervisory personnel received them, either they were not useful or changes were not reflected correctly. Although "our goal had been to shorten the billing cycle, we ended up expeditiously lengthening it to suit the kinds of problems we were encountering." In other cases, rather "than adjust labor to output, we would have to hire people to cope with whatever the output was." It was impossible to know "exactly where we stand, or if we're doing the best we can under the circumstances, or what."

The inaccessibility of reports posed another order of problems, in that "no one was where they were supposed to be, or at a desk or able to answer the phone. Everyone was wandering around, in the computer room aimlessly waiting on output, dipping into files, or running around trying to compile their own data because they couldn't wait any longer."

Data were not capable of being taken apart and recombined so that errors could be identified and learning incorporated back into the system. Recurring problems were not highlighted or were lost in the data shuffle. The control function was undermined, because supervisors were unable to trust the ability of workers to select appropriate responses and proceed accordingly. Time was spent "getting improperly prepared input properly reformatted, or getting the output just to make sense." Operations supervision became a function of coping rather than controlling.

The computer collapsed the function of management at the operations level, for in order to maintain minimal efficiency the supervisor actually had to take part in the work process she was supposed to be supervising. Supervision, in effect, was exchanged for first aid. When strategies are aimed at coping rather than controlling, the department operates in a costly state of crisis. The costs of both task-processing and personnel increased in financial services, as did the cost in terms of strain and demoralization.

DID THE REPORTS MEET THE NEEDS OF ANY?

Every department needed information with the characteristics of timeliness, accuracy, comprehensiveness, flexibility, proper aggregation, accessibility, and responsiveness to

change. No department got information with these characteristics. The dilemma is that even if a model could be designed to
produce information with the characteristics required by one
department, it could not meet the requirements of other users.

A "SOLUTION"

The solution to the hospital's problems was supposed to be
the MIS for financial management. It was envisioned as a
comprehensive MIS. It would use a large data base with interconnected subsystems that would in turn be built one upon the
other. The system designers knew that managers at different
levels needed different data, but they did not know what data
each manager needed, nor could they account for the conditions under which changes in data needs would occur. They had
some idea that if they collected as large and detailed a data base
as possible, if they tried to serve everybody with everything
that might conceivably be useful, and if they tried to make all
systems' parts good for everyone, then, inevitably, a multipurpose system useful to everyone would result.

What the hospital actually got was a system that not only
did not solve the original problems it was supposed to attack,
but created new ones. Managers still did not get the right data in
the right format at the right time. Now, however, instead of
having only the original problems to cope with, there was a new
set of problems, and managers had to deal with the problems
with both.

THE SOLUTION AS PART OF THE PROBLEM

The MIS was to be a solution to the hospital's problems of
financial management. It added new problems stemming from
the following.

1. Overcollection of data.   A large data base made for an over-abundance of data and an undersupply of information. Because managers got printouts composed of collections of recorded observations rather than data collected and arrayed according to their needs, which they would convert into information, the cost of making sense of these recorded observations fell upon the managers. Data were in the wrong scale or format, or did not even relate to the specific job. For example, when patients called to inquire about their bills, accounts could not be quickly found because billers had numerical rather than alphabetical account lists. Reports tallied with stages in the machine proc-ess but bore no relationship to the generally used accounting procedures.

As changes proliferated, reports became more confusing because managers were not sure that what they had learned from the past report held true for the current one. Because reports were late, productivity figures did not match up and therefore had to be completed manually. Departments that tracked productivity for professional reporting requirements found disparities between the professional/association reports and the financial income/expense reports, or personnel reports. Extracting certain data for personnel reports required sifting through the entire organization's personnel summaries. Finan-cial statements were often received several months late, so departments under or over budget could not adjust, since the quarter had passed. If departments kept their own records as a tally, the passage of time and error rate in the system report made reconciliation difficult, and after the passage of several months, even departments had difficulty recalling the details of circumstances that might account for disparities.

2. Interconnection of Subsystems.   Interconnecting all the subprograms not only posed logistical problems in that it be-came difficult if not impossible to extract one subsystem without running the entire data base; it was also expensive, since changes in one component necessitated changes in all others in order to stop error proliferation. Many data and many users mean errors get buried in masses of detail. They slip past one user, who counts on another to sort them out; but each user is sensitive only to what constitutes error in his or her own local-interest precinct, so errors pass through unrecognized as error. Errors that originated elsewhere are easily picked up and carried or aggregated into the operating bases of departments. The more error is hidden, the less likely it is to be corrected, and as a consequence, it can become embedded in programs far from the original source. The further the error travels, the greater becomes the cost of correcting it, since it has been imported into so many programs.

Interconnecting subsystems increase conplexity. Interconnected systems are complicated to work with. The large data base may set machine requirements above user needs, and error definition may become the property of system designers whose interests differ from those of managers. Designers wanted data capable of fitting easily into machine specifications, and managers wanted data capable of informing the multiple problem states and conditions they face. The costs of change, machine workability, and status deflation may become so high that the alternative of letting small errors through is preferable to updating reports endlessly, issuing correction lists, junking entire programs, or even going around telling everyone that the report's off, in error, sour again, or raising error tolerance levels. Furthermore, when the whole system is interconnected, opportunities for feedback are reduced because the system is just too large. Producers may never know the fate of the data they produce, and whether or not they are appropriate, while consumers may be so separated from producers that they have little chance to specify the data they wish or to correct them if they get something they do not want. Moreover, system operators intervene between producer and consumer. Interconnected subsystems are error-prone. When the output of one subsystem becomes the input of another, and so on, with all subsystems related to the whole, the system is vulnerable; if one part is mortally damaged, all the other parts are at risk.

When subsystems are interconnected across levels and boundaries, regardless of the differences in functions, distortion is introduced into the model; the separation between producer and consumer reduces the ability of one to estimate the validity of the other's data. A common error in billing, for example, was a confusion between ultrascan and ultrasound procedures. They were procedures from different medical departments, but recorded on the same type of charge slips. Poor handwriting made it impossible to distinguish the two. In the old days, when these charges were handled manually, if a department number was missing from the slip, the biller either recognized the handwriting or could call the department and ask for verification. The computer could not do this. Second, interconnected systems must generally meet tight standards for machine entry, because there is a limit, in a large model, to the operations and procedures the machine will accept. Data must be explicitly defined, with precise coding. In too many cases, however, the data will fall outside the category or code, requiring complicated hand entry, or else it has to be fudged into one or another category to expedite the processing. Machine efficiency and keeping the costs of operations down become paramount. For this reason, the DP staff may become the arbiters of what works, rather than management, which lacks the expertise to get the machines to perform.

3. Overdistribution of data. The system attempted to distribute most of the same data to everyone, irrespective of their needs or the fact that since the objectives of users were multiple, conflicting, and vague, there might not be relationships between the data and the decisions they needed to make. Inevitably, some objectives were fostered at the expense of others. Indicators relevant to the problems of some users were stressed at the expense of others.

Circulating the same data to everyone meant that many users got data in the wrong scale or time frame, too aggregated or too detailed. Data meant for one level were sent to levels where they were not particularly relevant. For instance, summaries of hospital personnel performance, including turnover

94 Simple Systems, Complex Environments

and sick-day rates, were regularly circulated to every department, even though departments had no particular interest in knowing why an employee left another department, since it had nothing to do with that department. In other cases, data arrived too early. Insurance and charge data that arrived before the patient record had been released, sat around or waited to be queued. Billers had to create special holding files and remember to correlate the file and the queue number and the rest of the patient billing data when all the bits got together. For others these data arrived too late to be useful. For example, the target level for the bad debt write-off was sent around after the cycle had been run and the machine had determined the level. However, the manager was supposed to set the level before the run. Users suffered from an exaggerated volume of data: Billers complained of being inundated with reports, addendums, statements, error lists, and updates, and complained they could not advise their clients because there was too much information to go through in order to get a straight answer.

In summarizing the effects of a multipurpose approach to information system development, the data-processing personnel inevitably look like the heavies in this scenario. It goes without saying that this is generally untrue, but what is true is that complex environments (1) that naturally function independently but are forced by external as well as technological requirements to function in an interdependent way, (2) that are linked together serially, so that a change in one component necessitates a change in every other one, (3) where incentives to cooperate are weak or nonexistent, and (4) where the primary information source requires verbal mediation, are not good candidates for multipurpose models. Either approach, to data base development — general pool or exception — results in a slow, heavy, and expensive model. The response of system designers is often to try to produce a model that represents the general features of most of the "shopping lists" users say they want. In reality, the model fails to reproduce any of these features in a useful and cost-effective way, and, what is more, it is error-prone, thereby causing further alternations in the behavior of organization members, as we will see next.

NOTE

1. The list of steps in this process was provided by the medical records supervisor at one of the hospitals. It may vary in other hospitals.

5 Coping with Error in Output

BOTH HOSPITALS' INTENTIONS in installing a computerized MIS were to get appropriate data to managers who made financial decisions. Yet, after costly and time-consuming adaptations to the system and many trial periods, it became increasingly clear that what was planned did not work, or worked only with difficulty. The consequence was that the MIS was not successful in meeting the needs of users.

When the system failed to perform with predictability, errors began to overload the organization, resulting in delays, backlogs, and arrearages, where problems at one managerial level or subsystem began to intrude upon other levels or subsystems.

When the MIS was unable to perform reliably, yet still carried the information actors needed to perform their work functions, they responded by "adapting" information produced in the system to fit their needs. Actors increased their tendency to set aside or amend previously established organizational rules and norms to conform with the demands of persistent anomaly in the MIS and the exigencies of organizational life.

Coping strategies are user-designed to deal with uncertainty by reshaping information to make it more nearly appropriate to

level these errors pose a risk, causing delay in recovery of money, and the longer it takes the hospital to collect the money owed to it, the more that money costs in terms of lost revenue, forgone income, or opportunity cost.

Errors (e.g., loss of control devices like operating statements) are high at departmental levels in terms of organizational conflict. Interpersonal relations between department managers and financial services disintegrated as financial services persisted in putting off statement delivery. For department managers, the loss of operating information — and in one year, the entire budget process — was damaging in that the department became subject to the risk of serious error in judgment and estimation of its resources. Department managers tended to rely more than usual upon intuition and experience in order to run their departments. However, when many departments react in a same or similar fashion, hospitals jeopardize quality control and growth and development opportunities.

The climate of error in part forced the manager of financial services to become the "invisible man"; he was constantly accosted in the halls over errors or found that he "had to be an apologist" for a system that he "had strongly opposed in the first place." He closeted himself in his office and relied on reports from his assistants. The hospital administrator and board of directors also had to cope with error, by creating their own alternative information systems. The detailed data routinely funneled up bore little relationship to the kinds of intelligence for strategic planning that managers need. Samples of typical errors at different levels follow.

1. Line Management. At the billing level, where the work was directed toward billing, collection, and accounting, typical errors were:

- *Late bills:* "Patient didn't get billed until months after he left the hospital, even though the account was submitted for processing five days after he left."
- *Inaccurate bills:* "A 63-year-old man received a bill for a Caesarian section."

- *Omissions:* "The bill was blank when the patient received it," or "needed to be amended four times until it was correct."
- *Machine errors:* "A change of address was submitted three times, and each time it was rejected and the bill was sent to the wrong address."
- *Sequencing errors:* "A patient received a collection notice before he received his bill."
- *Errors in entry:* "The computer did not drop the account into probate and automatic collection notices were sent to someone who was dead."

The result of these errors is that the patient is harassed and in turn "harasses the hospital or refuses to pay his bill." Billers must work harder to resolve output errors and work falls behind, because the billers are "always trying to clean up the past, get rid of the last headaches." The accounts receivable inventory grows, for it is still clogged with bills in error, which cannot be processed for collection. Furthermore, billers are tempted to write off small amounts more frequently than they normally might be, if only to get these accounts off their minds. They have little guidance from rules regarding debt write-offs, as rules vary widely. Nor do they have the guidance of a preestablished write-off level, because the level is established after the run, when the machine averages out losses. This means that the level serves as a post-factum justification rather than a decision rule. No one knows in advance how much is being written off or what total is being approached for a given period, because considerable time passes before the report is issued. When fifteen billers are writing off small annoyances, however, the cumulative effect over time may be a considerable loss for the hospital. The work backlog is cumulative, in that conflicting accounts more frequently pile up at the supervisory level, and the supervisor ends up "working like an overflow clerk" instead of as a line supervisor.

In a similar fashion, delay is likely to result when records are missing or incomplete. Billers may elect to put off the work necessary to render the accounts collectible until far into the future, or they may adapt records according to private systems which are not intelligible to anyone else or, for that matter, even necessarily correct. When individual accounts are in a state of disorder, the reporting of the account group is also going to be late or in error, requiring a number of correcting reports with additional delays. Furthermore, if the biller is away from work, no one else can make sense of the records.

2. *Other departments.* Problems were created in staffing and the ordering of necessary supplies: "The personnel budget had to be temporarily frozen just when we were so short-staffed we could hardly cope at all."

- *Conflict:* "If I could get my hands on the director. . . ." "We refuse to turn in any more charge data until they give us an operating statement."

- *Error:* "They charged another department's personnel budget to me twice in a row. The administrator saw only the deviance figure and almost took my head off before I could explain." "We had three days to prepare and submit our budget. Do you know how I did it? Took the annual rate of general inflation plus an estimated increase for the coming year and jacked up all my expenses by 7½% — including fixed and paid-for items. Then I added a figure on top to allow for my errors in estimation, plus another increment as a safety margin. I got it all."

3. *Financial Services Department Management.* Problems were created in *training:* "Training and retraining [as changes occur] sessions are taking up more time than we ever could have imagined."

- *Morale:* "Complaints, complaints, that's all there is to be heard around here."

- *Error:* "Budget deviations are running 35% - 40%, which certainly can't be right — or can it?" "The month's accounts don't tabulate with the daily census reports." "The computer picked

up the wrong technician-hour figure for that department."
"Gave them the wrong personnel budget figure." "Processed a
temporary load as a constant." "Applied the wrong pricing."

- *Inconvenience:* "The printout weighs about ten pounds. We
put tabs on the pages we need so that we can find them again. We
don't need the other pages. . . . I have no idea what those
columns mean; we ignore them."

- *Decisions preempted:* "The machine established the bad debt
write-off level according to the work it processed."

Department management was forced to intervene between
producers and consumers and between processors and consumers, and to act to resolve problems on the job, interpersonal
problems, and interdepartmental problems. The work flow distorted productivity so that management was capable of only
one response — to hire more people. It was forced to make
reports based on estimates or "eyeballing," because needed
data were delayed. Control was based strongly on system slack
and savings generated by strikes, ceilings on hirings, and management by past example. Since control over budgeting was
ineffectual without timely and accurate reports, management
had no ability to act in its primary capacity as financial adviser
(or controller) to intervene and change course where it was
necessary.

4. *Administrative management.* Reports were not useful to
the senior manager or the board of trustees. Typical problems
were:

- *Wrong format or scale:* "It is much more convenient as well as
efficient to have one of the assistants work up a brief report that
makes sense to the board, which just wants a general picture."

- *Insufficient filtering:* "There's no point in having a lot of detail
when much of the time the question is, 'How do we stand?' "

- *Not relevant:* "Most problems that concern us at this level fall
outside the hospital proper, in that they are community, government, regulatory or system problems."

The senior manager's response is to develop and rely upon a human information system capable of handling unique problems, as well as several different types of intelligence-gathering networks. In short, the system reinforces intuition, not only because it lacks relevance, but also because it contains unknown amounts of bias and distortion.

Along with coping with an environment characterized by a new and not always favorable set of interpersonal relationships, the organization must also deal with inadequacies in the information base: Data are late, of unknown origin, inaccurate, or in the wrong scale. When personnel finally resolve the access problem and finally get a report they need, they may have difficulty translating data into their own task or conceptual framework. For example, a biller, who wants to know what happened to a customer's last payment, does not want to hunt through all the last billing recaps. Worse, even after such effort, the data may do users no good at all, or may make things more difficult by causing users to seem inefficient or incompetent to the rest of the hospital departments.

None of the codes that is supposed to work, does. To get on with their work, actors must cause the system's output to meet at least some of their needs, if by doing nothing else but defending themselves against the system's encroachment upon their lives and sanity, to say nothing of their jobs. Struggling to cope with the system, actors employ a number of strategies in response to error and ambiguity (see Table 3). Typical stategies are:

- *Omission:* Leaving out information; failing to process data due to oversight, delay, or missing parts; not knowing what data to apply; or not having them handy or in an appropriate form.

- *Bypassing:* Going outside the official system, employing unstandardized calculations, regularly resorting to private information sources (usually knowledgeable persons) to find out "what actually happened."

- *Paralleling:* Using a "closet" system, a private, nonstandard manual, or replaced system to underwrite or secure the new

**TABLE 3   Strategies for Dealing with Uncertainty: Financial Services'
Reaction to Overload**

Subgroup	Relation to MIS	Behavior	Reason
INPUT PRODUCERS:			
Admitting	Initiate insurance data	Omission	Maintain departmental boundaries
Doctors	Sign off records	Omission, delay, escaping	Other priorities, suspect integrity of MIS in general
Other organizational departments	Billing and charge data inputs	Delay, error, escape	Other priorities, no reciprocity, no confidence, errors, do not see relationship to own interests
THROUGHPUT:			
Technical staff	Designers, agents of change	Queuing, omission, error, filtering, approximation	Other values
OUTPUT:			
AR personnel	Consumers	Error, omission, multiple channels, approximation, poor filtering	No confidence in MIS
Supervisory-managerial operations	Supervise and coordinate to meet externally as well as internally imposed criteria	Delay, multiple channels, approximation, poor filtering	Cannot get what they need
Managerial department	Responsible for implementation	Escaping, filtering	Have no confidence in MIS

one, on an ongoing basis, so that it is not merely functionally
redundant but absolutely essential to work performance.

- *Bootlegging:* Cutting categories of discrimination, guessing or
  estimating, making do with makeshift rather than specific reports, blurring, telescoping or collapsing categories and inter-

faces, fudging data into place, bootlegging data, altering print-outs.

- *Escape:* Not doing the task (e.g., not doing the necessary filing and paper-handling chores), refusing to use the system, reverting to old ways, projecting all the disabilities onto the system, deliberately withholding information, or committing sabotage.

- *Destroying priorities:* Destroying or throwing out altogether the small requests and lowest priorities, since there is not likely to be time or attention to devote to them. Giving easy problems first priority, difficult ones, last.

- *Reducing standards of performance:* Standards of performance are reduced in order to compensate for a spiraling error rate. The organization acts to save itself by accepting a large measure of error as inevitable. The reduced standard of performance is rationalized as "necessary under the circumstances" or "only temporary," and "will change when we get caught up" — but that does not happen.

THE MEANING OF STRESS TO THE ORGANIZATION

Errors, arrearages, and delays cause productivity to fall off steeply. There are potentially two different sets of behavioral responses (See Meir, 1961): I is *coping,* where strategies are employed to invent new problem-solving approaches. This stage is characterized by ad hoc corrective devices, and may under many circumstances permit the actors "to hang in while we try to think of something better." When coping strategies no longer work, however, *escape or breakdown* might be entered, in which actors perceive the situation as hopeless and act to save themselves from "going down" with the system.

Coping

The relationship between communications load and the appearance of stress follows a structured course: Ideal capacity cannot be obtained because of the increased error rate and obscuring of cause-and-effect relationships. The actors (system users) can no longer apply prearranged codes and formulas that were developed to match ideal conditions. However, there are no rules for coping with the disordered state of persistent error, or the less-than-ideal. In order to convert overload into units that can be processed, users must invent new sets of rules. These new rules are designed to be short-term problem solvers. They are invented for the purpose of resolving enough of the ambiguity to convert the information produced in the MIS into some form or other fit for consumption.

Defending

If the ambiguity in the system increases because of continual proliferation of error, coping strategies may no longer work, or error may outdistance the capacity of users to invent new strategies. The actors may now drop attempts to convert MIS information into ad hoc problem-solving forms and instead withdraw from the system entirely, via escaping or defending strategies. Sabotage is an extreme form of defense, where actors may actually attack the mechanical system, feed in random numbers, or destroy output. A more classic form of defense is denial, where the actor refuses to deal with the system or with the facts of the matter at all, (e.g., by not wanting to know about problems with the system), wishing to deal only "with the solutions" and/or insist that error is mechanical, not human. Another example of escape is "bailing oneself out," the "don't blame me" or "I told you so" syndrome.

COMMUNICATIONS CAPACITY

Ideal, coping, and *escape or defense* represent three degrees of communications capacity. Under the best of conditions, the ideal state may not be possible to achieve at all times and under all communications loads, because of flux from work volume and natural arrearages due to queuing in the system. However, the system has error-control devices available. It may drop to coping capacity temporarily, until the load crisis is resolved, which enables stress to be absorbed both by the temporarily reduced standard of performance and the assurance that the situation is temporary and life will be "back to normal" soon.

Under coping conditions, ideal behavior in terms of productivity and error-control standards has been set aside. Productivity is whatever is outputted, typified in such comments as "We're doing the best we can." Generally, a multiplicity of rules flourishes. Error correction is conducted as *reaction* to immediate and local disturbance. Relevance is lost as the pace of error increases. Multiple corrective strategies are applied, but since they are often topical, hasty, and local, they seldom become incorporated into the system. Furthermore, these strategies are so individual that other units seldom know what they are. Stress is magnified by the cumulative effect of a number of these individual responses. The system must now conduct itself in overload.

REASONS FOR ERRORS: WHY WAS DATA QUALITY POOR?

1. One reason was unevenness in the system. A multiplicity of procedures existed side by side, not all characterized by the same degree of development, some more elaborately specified, some described with far less precision, posing dilemmas of choice to users. The result was ambiguity.

> A common problem was trying to decide which procedure or code applied in individual cases, because there were two or three codes which were conceivable.

> If there wasn't a category, then what was one to do?

We really haven't got a standard set yet, so we usually take the same indicator last year as a comparison.

Well, I don't think that we're all using the same figure. It makes a difference if you average over the cycle, or over the quarter, and I think departments do pretty much what they want.

2. There was a lack of coincidence between established procedures and machine output, so coordination was difficult to achieve.

Accounts are out of balance with the system so it is difficult to enter update material.

Machine transfers and manual transfers do not always coincide, because we have difficulty telling the machine what we know, that the case is in dispute, probate, or whatever.

The government says do it this way, the system says do it that way; well, I only know one way to do it, and it isn't either of those two.

3. There were coding ambiguities. When models are large and complex, it is necessary to define entry procedures narrowly. Thus, procedures are rigid and cannot encompass enough variety. This presents a problem for "deviant," "slightly deviant," and "mostly deviant" material which does not fit nicely into the preestablished categories. On the other hand, if the case is coded "deviant," it might not get processed until after the run is completed, holding up an entire report for users.

We fudge the data into categories, I admit it.

We make a few modifications so that we don't have to sit around on a report.

You may have to guess a little on the categories.

The ones they give us are not quite right, but they're not quite wrong, either, so you have to guess.

4. There was no easy system to correct small or common errors, so users were not willing to go through long, complicated systems, particularly if they knew that there would be further changes on the account in the near future.

No, we don't process deviations as we get them. We usually save them up and do them all on one day. The reason is that it's necessary to first find the original report, update and date it and indicate what's wrong, find the error list, update it, then see if the cases are on that, and change it accordingly. Tell the system, go through the files — you can see what a long, complicated process it is.

It is usually better to change the error by hand on the printout. Otherwise, you need to make out an entry form, with a system notice. Then you get back the original entry form, a correction sheet, amended reports, and about a dozen printouts for each account, and still the report might be in error.

We need categories numbered from 8 to 11, but the system can only accommodate one-character classes, so we keep our own private system rather than have to cram data into their classes.

5. Another reason data quality was poor was lateness of data. Reports were often not available in time to serve the needs of the decision makers.

I would say that only on one occasion was the statistical report and graph of performance ready in time for the board meeting.

It does little good to try and answer patient inquiries, since the report isn't here to check out the account.

The data in the reports are pretty old by the time they get here.

They run part of the report; then problems develop so you may have to wait around to get the other part of it.

6. The system becomes encumbered by data waiting on tests to develop options to follow, on data waiting for completion, or data which require analysis. When one level cannot produce, other people wait around for their reports. In a large system those at one end of the data chain may have little opportunity or ability to influence others to get their reports in.

> Well, their secretary is on vacation, so they can't do the report until she comes back.

> The report didn't get signed off because the head of the department is out ill.

> They have new regulations, so we will just have to wait until they figure out how to comply and make their report.

7. Procedures that facilitate one subsection inconvenienced other subsections. Various units were disadvantaged by errors that did not even originate with the data.

> DP has a three-day leeway in which to run the cycle. This means that you never know in advance exactly when bills will come out. It also means that you may have very short notice to get your stuff in on time.

> It is easier for the system to track on the basis of age, so accounts get kicked into categories where they might not really belong, simply because they fulfill the age test.

> Errors are listed in separate reports, so if you don't have the correcting report, and if it isn't dated and numbered, you're really up the creek.

> I usually wait to do the report, to make sure that all the corrections have been issued.

When each department had its own form, the lack of standardization "required billers to expend extra amounts of work 'reading' each form." Yet, once a master form was developed, "there were complaints that it wasn't suitable here or there, or what have you." As an efficiency measure, financial services tried a form that could be used by the professional services units, but here they ran into trouble: "A common problem was that some similar-sounding procedures were confused, even though they belonged to two different departments — physical therapy and nuclear medicine — and it might take days to find errors like this."

Whenever a change took place in a form, even departments that were not directly affected by the change might have had to revise their whole form system, or at least adapt it to fit the new format. Adaptations might take place "just after a department got to the point where it could use the form efficiently — and had ordered a year's supply of forms."

8.   Data were biased. Because information systems channel data from personnel from one organizational level to another, users may have no interaction with data providers. Thus, if they question the data, it is not so easy to go directly to the provider and find out what the user needs to know.

> Operating costs are difficult to arrive at. Some departments count noses, some rely on accounting records, but errors in these records challenge the credibility. If you don't know which way a department is counting, then you can't estimate how off they are. If there isn't time to go find the department, there's trouble.
>
> The charges could be so far off. If you know who is making out reports, then you have some idea of how accurate they are. For example, there are certain wards which never list all their charges because they get busy or forget; others are fairly accurate. You really need to get people on the phone and ask them how they did something.
>
> Of course those figures are off. The trick is to find out by how much they're off.

Systems become difficult to control, for the data base is large, reports are numerous, and time is short. Speed is important, and there are extensive charges, all of which pose obstacles to the rationality of users.

ERROR SYSTEMS BECOME ORIENTED TO CORRECTION RATHER THAN CONTROL

A system of corrections aims to control the consequences of error, while a system of control aims to search and eradicate the causes of error. As long as a MIS has only correcting capacity, the same errors will happen over and over, because they never get detected and removed. Control capacity is essential. Control capacity may not become fully developed, because the pressures of getting the reports produced means that systems people may not get time to search and analyze, so they try to patch up as they go along.

Because systems people were busy, financial services people uncertain, and problems numerous, systems changes were extensive. Often the same problem was solved over and over again, because no one had taken the time to write down the steps involved in the change or to rewrite the program so that the same error would not recur. Many times it was not possible to find out "that something wasn't really working out until it was running on the machine."

To save time, the system of batch control was directly transferred from the previous manual system. Batches were sorted, totaled, numbered, and logged for submission, but "because of the way the system operates, batches are combined and errors rejected on three separate reports." Consequently, there was no way to tie the error back or to verify the small batches that were originally submitted.

In a similar example, the system of errors correction was oriented toward steps in the processing procedure, which made sense only to processors. An error list was generated for each step, however, and circulated so that users could update their reports; still, "the formatting did not match the reports to be updated." Not only were financial services people completely bewildered; the list was completely useless to them.

WHAT ERROR MEANS TO THE HOSPITAL ORGANIZATION

Weick says that organizational environments are "enacted." It is entirely possible that, instead of adapting to a ready-made environment, the actors *themselves* create the environment to which they adapt: "Rather than talking about adapting to an external environment, it may be more correct to argue that organizing consists of adapting to an enacted environment, an environment which is *constituted* by the actions of interdependent human actors." In short, organizations are *proactive*. They create as well as constitute their environments. Therefore, if actors act irrationally, they create an irrational environment (Weick, 1969: 27).

OVERLOAD AS A FRAMEWORK FOR ADAPTATION

What does it mean to say an organization creates an *irrational environment?* It would be more proper to ask first, what a rational environment is. Under conditions of rationality, there exist programs, sets of formulas or maps, that enable members to make sense of the space in which they find themselves. They know "what stimuli to respond to, when, and how to respond, and under what conditions they may alter or modify responses. They have no special difficulties encoding and they have little trouble in exchanging with their environment." However, the conditions necessary to maintain rationality can disintegrate: "The unexpected appears — if there should arise persistent anomalies and sustained discrepancies between normal expectations and actual outcomes, the fit is broken. The usual things do not work anymore and we are in trouble" (Landau, 1969).

Landau warns that, for the organization's actors, the "strains imposed can be too much, the burden of error can be too great — in short, he can be overloaded." The consequence is an environment where uncertainty is amplified up and down the organizational lines. The difference now, however, is that there is not only the original condition of uncertainty, which sent the organization in search of a solution (an information system as an answer) in the first place; there is also the added condition of uncertainty caused by the system itself. The MIS is a solution, then, which has become its own problem. Since the solution makes no sense, individual rationality dictates that we make sense out of it by trimming it to fit needs, so we can get on with life.

The control of error requires a more practical understanding of human and organizational behavior. Error control eschews linear, serial, interdependent, and unique concepts of design, and substitutes instead duplication, overlap, and redundancy, to increase the possiblity of outcomes going right (as well as to decrease the risk of failure in parts) and to protect the organization from disastrous breakdowns, while still permitting learning to proceed (Landau, 1969).

ORGANIZATIONS AS KNOWLEDGE-PRODUCING ENTITIES

Formal organizations are founded on the exercise of control on the basis of knowledge. Organizations possess or are capable of producing the knowledge necessary for their tasks. They are, as Landau (1973) puts it, "knowledge-producing agents." That is, the structure of an organization contains the repository of knowledge deemed necessary for reaching the goals that legitimate the organization's existence. Landau goes on to suggest that the organization's structure constitutes a memory bank consisting of knowledge of cause-and-effect relations, from which derive the rules, regulations, and formulas for dealing with the task environment.

Analogous to the structure, function consists of the activities of members of the organization to test the structural knowledge of the organization against the task environment, as well as to acquire information about the real world that is capable of altering the organization's funded knowledge. An effective interchange over time between funded and acquired knowledge is one form of organizational learning. Change without violent oscillation constitutes "the self-correcting organization," in Landau's words (1973), while the opposite stereotype would be the self-ossifying organization, that is, the organization that substitutes authority for performance test and screens out all challenges to its dogma. Landau predicts that in the absence of learning, an organization would collapse.

Over time, the knowledge supplied to an organization's initial structure becomes altered or amended as a consequence of functioning in a changing environment — provided that the organization is able to learn from what it does. Without error there would be no learning, for error denotes a surprise in fit between codes or calculations and tasks, at the point where information exchange takes place. Normally, when there is a good fit between inputs and outputs, things run smoothly and are, within acceptable limits, predictable. On the other hand, "if the unexpected appears, if there should arise persistent anomalies and sustained discrepancies between normal expectation and actual outcome, the fit has been broken. The usual things do not work anymore, the situation has become disordered" (Landau, 1973).

The organization must move to reorder the task environment with new problem-solving strategies. The organization is supposed to be able to use its MIS for the purpose of uncovering and understanding error. The MIS is supposed to perform this function by converting data into information. Data become information by participating in a system or theory that organizations manipulate to produce knowledge. If theory about the complex interactions of policy were available and if organizations were willing and able to use it, information would be produced, errors uncovered, and new knowledge supplied by examination of the interrelations among functions (Wildavsky, 1979).

In the social domain, however, theory is weak or even nonexistent. In the organizational domain, the will to change may be weak or missing altogether. If knowledge and will are not conjoined, then change may not necessarily follow the perception of a disorder. The MIS is weak in theory and it cannot compel the will to act, so it lacks a fully developed error-sensing function. Without a basis of knowledge, the MIS may be insensitive to change in the task environment. Furthermore, in the absence of a knowledge base capable of producing rules and reducing environmental variety in decision rules, the MIS may actually create so many internal errors that the larger errors between the organization and its environment become obscured or overlooked.

The primary task of the information system is to provide data at a reasonable cost with sufficient accuracy and timeliness. Users complained, however, that the MIS produced data there were low in quality and late. As a result, managers had little confidence in the data derived from the system, and were unwilling to depend on them. As we will see next, more often than not these data are not useful for management decision-making.

6 Problems of Producing Information

THE COST, QUALITY OF CARE, AND ACCESSIBILITY of services to the community are matters of ongoing concern to the hospital administrator. The adminstrator would like to know how well or poorly the organization is performing, what deviations from standards exist, and where in the system problems might exist. Much data relative to these concerns are available within individual hospital units, and are supposed to find their way into the information system, where a series of complex operations are supposed to convert them into information for the health care executive to use in the management of the organization.

Unfortunately, most of the data are not useful for management decision-making. They consist of summaries or aggregations of other data. They are in the wrong time frame or at the wrong level of detail, pertain to matters that are outside the managers' control or are entirely unavailable or unresponsive to the questions to which they are addressed:

(1) The traditional paradigm of organizational levels was not useful for relating management task and control function.

(2) The information produced was not action-oriented.

(3) The organization was treated as independent of the organization.

THE HOSPITAL'S INFORMATION NEEDS

The hospital must produce information capable of responding to five general dimensions: patient information and billing, labor management, financial analysis, and accounts payable, and medical performance and review. These areas must be summarized along a time frame ranging from weekly to semiannual or annual report sets if the hospital is to control its activities. An example of monthly areas follows.

- A/R trial balances
- revenue and usage reports
- physicians' utilizations
- labor management: budget variances, new hires, terminations, utilization statistics, departmental costs, payroll, trend analysis
- revenues and expenses: balance sheet, income/expense statement, general ledger
- reimbursement: contracts, allocations, statistical analyses, audits
- basic hospital reports: activity, indexes, discharge, death registers
- medical statistical reports: service analyses, length of stay summaries
- utilization review activity
- reports and profiles, activity

AT THE DEPARTMENT LEVEL

The need to know about these areas can be expressed in terms of the following ongoing concerns:

(1) billing and accounting of patient accounts, operational summaries

(2) analysis of account activity

(3) maintaining and updating price lists, producing reports on the hospital's anticipated income over several categories

(4) accounting the general ledger along with the accounts payable and a series of financial, operating, and budget statements

(5) producing reports to auditors, tax consultants, creditors, and various government agencies

(6) preparing budgets, projecting costs and consumer demands into long-range policy

(7) producing management reports

(8) planning development

(9) evaluating financial performance

(10) analyzing productivity and planning for the future

(11) preparing third-party insurance reports

(12) conducting ongoing service audits

(13) cost-control reports

(14) work force productivity, staffing reports

INFORMATION REQUIREMENTS

To perform these functions, the information system would need the capability to summarize past behavior in absolute figures, in ratios, and in trends across a series of indicators. It would have to be capable of predicting change in supply and demand and then incorporating those changes into a model to forecast short- and long-range futures on another level. If predictions about the future are to be meaningful, the organization must relate to its environment in a sensitive way, for if predictions are wrong — say, if the hospital changes in service-area composition, and these changes go undetected — there are important implications for the organization's survival. If, for example, the hospital begins to take in a steeply increased percentage of Medicare patients, it might have to consider revising its service capacity to fit the needs of a changing population group. If it were suddenly to take in a much larger percentage of Medicare patients, then it might have to think about revising its pricing formulas, for it would suddenly be operating on the premise that most patients will be acutely rather than chronically ill, that they will not stay in the hospital very long, that they will be insured or able to support the costs of their hospital stay personally. This means that the hospital needs to know what is going on in the local community, the changes that will affect the hospital. Our hospital misread signals in the environment and took a temporary increase in the local birthrate to signify a long-term change. It added an obstetrics unit and then found utilization dropping steeply, since the increased birthrate was only temporary. It had to close the unit. On the other hand, it underestimated the demand for a 24-hour pediatric service and then learned that it was losing many patients to facilities that could offer such a service, so it quickly began to expand its pediatrics unit. Therefore, if the organization is to be able to plan with accuracy, strategic planning needs information that is for the most part externally rather than internally derived, that is, varied and broad in scope.

THE DEPARTMENT MANAGER

The primary interest of the department manager is the hospital's financial assets and whatever can affect them, how the departments are doing in managing resources, and whether or not the people the manager has chosen to supervise various subsystems of the hospital's financial operations are doing what they are supposed to be doing. There is one major question about operations: How much income is the hospital generating in relation to its commitments? The answer lies in knowing the monthly level of accounts, their dollar value, the distribution of credits and debits, and some dimensions along averages,

categories, time span, and projections, in comparison to different time states.

A lot of the manager's time is taken up in supervising the
collection of Medicare and Medicaid accounts, and in making
sure the appropriate audits are performed. There are such
questions to resolve as, "Is the fiftieth percentile of the length
of stay the same as the average length of stay?" The manager
will sign completed audits and answer for the information the
audits contain. Reporting on the wrong indicators can cause the
patient-stay days to vary considerably, distorting the hospital's
care profile. In many cases, "somewhere down in the system or
in a department, someone may have arbitrarily chosen a figure
to resolve a temporary ambiguity or smoothed a situation to
expeditiously make things appear better than they really are.
By the time I see the completed audit, I probably have no idea
where it's coming from." Other times, "the fiscal intermediary
will wish to discuss lengths of stay, an overutilization problem
she sees, but I just can't put my hands on the right information,
because it's not outputted in a way that responds to her questions" or it would "take days to get." This "disadvantages [the
manager] in negotiations with her. I need that information to
protect us. There she sits with a computerized pattern-of-care
profile of our hospital in front of her, and I can't even find the
figures to defend our policies. . . . We have them. The question
is where the hell in the organizaiton are they?"

The manager is also interested in the relationship between
physician activity and revenue to be attributed to that activity.
Costs per procedure are tabulated and supplied to physicians
with signifant deviations from the average indicated. The purpose is to identify clinical practices that show significant deviations in order to assess the impact of this behavior. There "were
problems in producing this information for monthly departmental analyses, because we were so overwhelmed doing our external reports that DP could only run these when they had
completed the more essential reports . . . too late for most
departments." The "M D committees would get ideas about
figures they'd like to see in a report, and when we finally were

able to produce these, they'd say 'oh, interesting' and toss the thing aside. They no longer had any interest in it." When the deviation report was produced, "we had the 'so-what' problem. How were we to get individual doctors to change their behavior? That was up to their committee. In any case the doctor could always say that he was doing his best for a patient or the report was all out of proportion." In some cases "the guys responsible for the most deviations also brought in the most business." Other times, they would say, "Well, it's the nurses' fault, lab's — whatever."

Personnel staffing reports were "supposed to help us hold down labor expenses and establish staffing patterns." In reality, "nursing staffing patterns were determined within the unit itself and, as far as I know, the monthly report on hours worked per patient day bore no relationship to any nurse-patient ratio in effect." If there was "a cost-effective staffing ratio established in one unit, it didn't coordinate with the lab's or radiology's, so the nurses had to wait on other departments to get their work done." Reports were not useful at the department management level.

The model could not reliably produce trending. The report was "only produced after all the others, and it was always late, because someone forgot to rewrite the program." In fact, "it was produced as an afterthought, if someone had the time." Reports arrived late, long after targets had been established. We often produced them "by eyeballing or using the past month's performance as an indicator." "Many targets were pretty much established by the computer in relationship to how much work it had left to process or by using arbitrary target dates." Large "personnel-to-workload indicators made no sense, because it wasn't possible to tell if they were due to a sudden crisis or were going to be around for a while." Similarly, such reports as average day's revenue were "misleading because of the backlog in unprocessed accounts or those missing parts from other departments."

Reports were insufficiently aggregated for the management function because they were essentially summaries of "what

everyone else in the office got," or they were "summaries of
other people's summaries." In order to be useful, an assistant
had to recompile them, but the process of recomputation introduced considerable, if unknown, bias and distortion into the
report. Compilation was produced "under pressure of demand
and circumstances, and a number of people might work on
different parts of the reports," which meant they lacked standardization and could not be compared with each other reliably.

Unable to determing what, exactly, the manager wanted,
supervisors supplied what they thought might be needed.
"Whatever supervisor made up the monthly report tended to
emphasize parts she knew and understood and downplay parts
she wasn't interested in." Over time the requirements of a
particular subsystem came gradually to dominate the needs of
the total system.

Reports were not useful because even at their best they
could only produce quantitative information. The model could
not collect and report on such goals as quality in order to
answer questions such as, "If more money is in the accounts
receivable, and if the hospital is processing more patients, is the
quality of service the same as, more than, or less than that at a
previous time and condition?" or "What would be the effect if
the percentage of Medicaid patients in proportion to the total
hospital patient population were to increase?" Yet, managers
would be interested in questions such as these in order to
explain how well they were doing or their departments were
likely to do, given certain changes, over the future.

The reports were not comprehensive, in that little commonality existed to link reports to common denominators. (Even
the accounts receivable and accounts payable reports were
produced independently.) Physician practice deviations were
tracked only in relation to a procedure and a cost unit rather
than in terms of a physician's overall revenue production.
Accounts receivable was always so far behind that "the general
ledger was produced in arrears." The report might be so in error
that "the only one who could figure it out was the chief ac-
countant, who — wisely — was never around here." Increasing

the conjuction between the two principal subsystems would have meant "increasing computer processing time, and the cycle was already being lengthened to the point where financial health might be jeopardized." The manager could complain, but he "had little success in changing the situation because he couldn't articulate his needs precisely enough. . . . Assistants and DP people tried to give him what they'd want if they were in his place. . . . The more data they gave him, the more he seemed to ask for." Unfortunately, for the most part this turned out to be more formal activity recaps, and this was "precisely what he didn't want."

The actual report was either significantly different from what physicains said they wanted and would use, or was produced so late that physicians had lost interest in it by the time it arrived.

THE ADMINISTRATOR

It is worthwhile to take a more detailed look at the administrator's function, for the administration of this hospital has evolved in a short time from caretaking (keeping the plant in relative order) to managing (planning and controlling a health care system). The information needs of the administrator have increased proportionately.

THE FUNCTIONS OF THE ADMINISTRATOR

The definitive characteristic of the administrator's work is, in the words of our administrator, "its political aspect." The administrator functions at the interface of the organization and its environment, between professional sectors, organizational levels, political groups. His or her skills are dependent on an ability to articulate preferences within an organizational framework, so that the proper questions get addressed by the proper resources and individuals.

Because of time constraints, the administrator relies heavily on concise, preferably "statistical or tabular summaries" and verbal data, many from a multiplicity of sources that are best described as intelligence sources. This intelligence supports one of the most essential functions, the building of strategies to achieve future goals. Many questions the administrator addresses are interrelated with other issues, and take time to develop into questions that can be related directly to the future, attempting to anticipate problems, especially financial pitfalls.

In order to assess the impact of the information system upon the work of the administrator, we must first try to understand what it is that the administrator does. Mintzberg (1973: 4) asserts that managers' jobs are remarkably alike:

> [The] manager is . . . both a generalist and a specialist. In his own organization he is a generalist — the focal point in the general flow of information and in the handling of general disturbances. But as a manager he is a specialist. The job of managing involves specific roles and skills. Unfortunately we know little about these skills.

Administrators see their basic function as "supervising the hospital's discharge of its obligations with regularity and reliability on a day-to-day basis." They are concerned "that the organization adapt to change in an orderly fashion." Since administrators serve at the discretion of the community, they must see that their organizations meet those prespecified ends. They translate the general guidelines and goals of the board of trustees into "specific operational strategies conducive to the hospital's framework."

Administrators are responsible for ensuring that the hospital deliver quality health care safely and efficiently. They are fully prepared to modify the definition of patient care in nontechnical ways and to interpret the institutional commitment of the hospital to the community it serves.

Administrators are assisted by assistant administrators as well as administrative assistants, each a specialist in a field such as nursing or business administration. In addition, our hospital also employed independent consultants in public relations and long-range financial planning, although it planned to discontinue the use of independent consultants "as soon as the MIS functions fully." The assistant administrators are responsible for such fields as development, patient care, and professional relations. They oversee and manage various divisions of the hospital's operations.

The administrator is called upon to reconcile a number of political forces acting upon (as well as within) the hospital: interest groups in the community that want the hospital to serve "particular health needs," groups "intent upon the growth and development of the hospital as well as groups not so intent." There are also frustrations from government and planning agencies that interpret the hospital's goals differently, and "of course the conflicting aims and desires of various components of the medical staff." Legislative and regulatory constraints, licensing requirements, and local planning body determinants of bed need are additional constraints. Administrators spend most of their time in formal meetings with directors, trustees, influential community groups, and medical representatives, where they negotiate with pressure groups or explain the hospital. They see themselves as spokespersons; that is, "many groups in the community encounter the hospital through [the administrator], and of course, it works the other way, too, in that the hospital encounters community preferences through [the administrator], as the board's representative. The administrator stands "between the community and the organization, with obligations to both." Like managers in other institutions, administrators are subject to pressures exerted from below in the organizational hierarchy as well as from above, because the two lines of authority in the hospital require continued renegotiation of the organization's order at different levels, and what cannot be resolved below filters up to the administrative level.

Mintzberg (1973: 4) describes managerial work as distinguished by quantity, variety, fragmentation, and brevity. These characteristics appear to fit the administrator's work accurately.

1. The day "begins early and there is considerable work. Meetings and obligations extend into the evening." A steady stream of callers go in and out. "All working hours of the day are scheduled, including lunch, which is always a hospital-related meeting."

2. "A number of issues recur — in different guises, or different problem forms, just when you think you've resolved them." However, most problems are "unique," and "very few are what [one would] call routine in the usual sense of the word, except regularly scheduled meetings."

3. The time the administrator can devote to any single issue is brief and "likely to be interrupted by something else." Because of the demands on administrators' time, their attention must be switched to different issues and problems before they get a chance to fully develop a problem.

4. Our administrator can only give short periods to problems and people at any given time. He often "gently urges people to come to the point" in meetings, and expresses a dislike for "long memos or calls." Attempts are made to screen out and reroute whatever can be handled by another executive. The administrator has finally decided to curtail many of the contacts he formerly "enjoyed with department heads, for I no longer have time, and there are other executives available." However, when he wants something from one of his subordinates, he "does not hesitate to bypass the hierarchy and go directly to the source."

He thinks about money-related problems and "running as tight a ship as possible," which is becoming "increasingly difficult with the rate of inflation in the hospital sector what it is." He believes that "all hospitals have basically the same problem, and that is "how to stay in business and how to keep everyone happy." When he is thinking about money, he is "thinking in terms of rather distant future states, of attracting large donations, interesting the community in underwriting expansion programs, or attempting to figure out what our needs will be several years ahead." Hospital planning is inevitably future-oriented because there is considerable distance between the time money is committed to the hospital and the time it actually comes into the hospital. "You always have to be ready to exploit advantages when they occur."

THE ADMINISTRATOR AND INFORMATION

Administrators, like most managers, do not have long periods of uninterrupted time at their disposal. Furthermore, they prefer "action to reflection" and like very much being "involved actively." From time to time our administrator has need for intensive ("about 20 minutes") examination of documents, such as end-of-the-month statements, where he is "primarily looking for trends of department performances." He can inhibit organizational development by postponing authorization requests, by delaying improvement projects, by reducing the amount of information he disseminates. "Time," he notes, is his "major limiting factor. There is simply never enough."

The lack of available time affects the ways in which he processes the information he gets for decision. In Mintzberg's opinion, getting information quickly appears to be more important to the manager than getting it completely right. Speculation and informal conversations are large parts of the administrator's information. The administrator says that he learns "a lot talking to people in the halls, to key individuals." He maintains an extensive network both in and out of the organization and claims to make use of it — for example, in monitoring doctors. The doctors are directly charged with monitoring themselves through the appropriate professional committee, but the administrator, in his position as agent of the board of directors, is responsible for developing contacts to help him to appraise medical performance informally, as an outside guide to how well the medical sector is actually functioning. He says he does not want more information; in fact, he is "trying to keep it from coming up here except under emergency circumstances." Because of the limits on his time and his desire to concentrate on long-range planning, he would prefer the hospital to be "as decentralized as is both efficient and possible" and to resolve its problems at department or division level, coming to his office only if problems cannot be resolved.

The administrator prefers "short, concise and clearly written information" when he requests it, but this written information may be, at least in part, conveyed to him verbally or filtered through his assistants in frequent meetings. He says he has a preference for this kind of information: "I often don't know what I want far enough ahead of time, and then when I want it, I need to get it immediately." It is much easier to pick up the telephone and call an assistant than to go through a MIS report or create a new one from scratch. He refers to his assistant as "well-informed," "creative," able to provide "rapid turnaround," "confidential," and "accurate."

By necessity, he keeps a lot of things in his head. Issues begin in the past and extend far into the future, or can be influenced by the opinions of major contributors or strong medical staff members. As the adjustment between preferences and resources unfolds, the administrator's informational needs change. Once he knows what he needs, he may go directly to the source or get his assistants to work on it. However, in the course of the question-developing period, he will often ask his assistants to develop information on expected outcomes and costs of a possible decision. He has to consider the impact of a decision on other decisions as well as on the hospital and the organization's overall goals. Decisions have to be acceptable to the hospital's influencers, and they have to accord with available resources. It is not enough to know the costs and benefits of a proposed solution; there must be a realistic sense of feasibility and of risk as well.

THE ADMINISTRATOR AND FINANCIAL INFORMATION

The financial information reporting system was designed to culminate in the administrator's office (as well as in the appropriate board committees). Since the administrator "thinks about money much of the time and most of his conversations in one way or another concern money," would a financial MIS be useful to him? The reports planned to work off the system were never produced in their planned form, as comparative graphs showing trends on changes and performance against overall hospital objectives, for the objectives turned out to be "either too complex or too simplistic to articulate meaningfully," and then it turned out that the computer could not graph the charts without an expensive and complicated reconversion. Once or twice the reports were produced by hand, but "they were too old to be useful." For example, one chart was supposed to show projected bad debt write-offs and anticipated losses against income, "but by the time [the reports] were produced, the period they were analyzing had come and gone, so if we were going to intervene, it was too late." The reports were never sufficiently comparative with any objectives, as it turned out: "They were very nude figures" that could have been obtained from the end-of-the-month report, which was also forwarded to the administrator.

To be useful at the executive level, reports must be capable of "showing trends and ratios in order to give a general picture of the status of the whole hospital." To analyze the operation as a whole, dollar figures are not useful, because they are neither comparative across specialty lines nor useful in projections. The hospital is expanding, but it is interacting in a highly competitive environment, and "we are all trying to attract the best specialists around." There "would be no point, however, if we couldn't provide the support services they need." "It's important to know how departments are doing in comparison to different workloads, so we know if we need to change and how."

The monitoring needs of managers are not likely to be too well served by centralized information systems, since much of the intelligence, and often many of the coercive strategies, are missing from a MIS, either because of the confidentiality of the data or the inability to encompass them within the MIS framework. For example, in reviewing the budget and the personal motivation it engenders, contractual departments, which receive percentages of the gross, will be more motivated than those which don't. But there are some considerations that make other kinds of information more effective. The medical laboratory, for example, receives not only a negotiable percentage of the gross it generates, but part of that is delivered in unattached discretionary funds. It is to its advantage to maximize income as much as possible and simultaneously minimize its expenses, particularly by keeping the costs of its technology low. However, not only does this raise a problem for administrative control due to embedded error levels, but there is also a considerable organizational strain caused by the workload on departments that must do support services for the lab. Finally, there are salary increases and professional increments linked to the medical laboratory's gross income formula. Stategies other than expense and income must be found in order to convince the pathologist to be happier with less, so to speak. While the MIS is capable of providing some of the information the executive needs to monitor the organizaiton effectively, it leaves out much that is important in helping him *understand* the performance of the total organization.

DISSEMINATING

The administrator says that it is very easy for people in the organization to stop him in the halls and ask him a question. He adds that it is easier for him to give them an answer than not, since most of what they want to know is in his head. This practice is an outgrowth of the time when the organization was small. While the administrator would now like to discourage this practice, he says that he has not yet found a way. The information the manager disseminates to the organization falls into recurring categories:

(1) General history: The "we last tried that in 1968" variety. It was /was not a good idea for these reasons.

(2) General recommendations: "If I were you, I'd go for A over B."

(3) Psychological support: "You have a good idea there," "looks great," or "don't worry."

(4) Confidential advice: "If you do that, then you're going to be hooked into supporting X or Y, whether you want to or not."

In terms of information for dissemination, the administrator dispatches problem-solving aids, generally rather than specifically formatted, rather vague, often psychological or supportive in thrust, frequently confidential, and, from time to time, disapproving. To his subordinates the administrator gives out much information that cannot easily be detached from his person. In fact, he himself believes that the face-to-face contact and solidarity purposes of his information role are so important that no information system could be as effective. In short, he believes that the interaction rather than the specific information is what has benefit.

STRATEGY-MAKING

Wildavsky (1974: 153) describes strategy-making as complex and adaptive. Managers tend

to break their projects for improvement into a series of sequential decisions because of their need for timing and feedback. Neither their search for, nor their evaluation of, alternatives appears to be conducted according to systematic design, and organizational values are applied to decisions which in some manner remain mysterious.

In strategy-making, the good manager makes use of programs to learn what works, and moves from iteration and interaction, trying different hypotheses according to each change in circumstances. Can a centralized system be useful to the executive's information needs in strategy-making? The importance of the executive's ability to perceive rather vague preferences and translate them into problems capable of resolution is considerable, as is the need to reconcile what he himself calls "the active political element."

Although only the basic duties of the administrator are considered here, it is clear that he supervises and coordinates the services and procedures that constitute the output of the organization, and ensures that each unit has sufficient resources to effect its contribution to the total effort. In turn, the administrator negotiates and facilitates the organization's exchange with the environment and attemps to iron out difficulties that threaten to impair that exchange. He is charged with keeping down the consumption of resources and with actively engaging in activites that foster the acquisition of more resources.

Each time the administrator seeks information, he is looking for something beyond what is ordinarily conveyed in a MIS — he is trying "to get a sense," "a feel for," "an understanding of." For example, there are many aspects of the finance and budgeting program that interest the administrator, for he must deal with the difficulty of weighing requests for allocations from competing programs, from individuals who are practiced in manipulating credibility. There are always many demands and always limited resources. Most of the time the administrator must make judgements about competing demands, "although he lacks basic information or technical knowledge of the proffered alternatives," and in fact, no information exists.

Most computer-based MIS treat the executive level of management as if problems were specific and search techniques developed, a condition that may, under certain circumstances, obtain on the operations management level, but seldom do on the executive, where uncertainty is great and problems are unformulated, related to other problems, and difficult to solve.

PROBLEMS IN MANAGEMENT AND INFORMATION

1. The problem of organizational levels. In the nature of things, data producers and data consumers are not equally situated in regard to the need for data. Within the same organizational level, perceptions of requirements may alter demands faster than conversion can supply information, since rapid revisions of needs arise in response to situations. Unsatisfied or distrustful of what is sent up to the organization, consumers may respond by asking for more data. More summaries of other summaries are sent up, with each level filtering the data, adding its own particular bias until most detail is eliminated and order is added in the data-compression effort. Lower levels add good intentions: They send up what "knowledgeable" sources think the executive wants. Unattractive or awkward features are smoothed out. Absence of direct feedback or incentives to producers means that producers may never know the effect of the data they produce. Inference rather than message moves up the organizational chain. In this fashion, the top of the organization stipulates its needs for information, but the lower levels actually create the decision elements.

2. Strategies for Coping with Inadequate Information. Just as managers of business firms have developed considerable expertise in adapting to informational inadequacies, the hospital administrator has quickly found strategies of his own. He makes use of critical indicators: patient census, admissions and discharges, patient charges, surgery schedules, cash flow, and who is "in the house" (for special attention). Information on these indicators can be transmitted verbally and quickly. It need not be accurate, only approximate.

3. The Problem of Information without Orientation. Mangers may not know what they want, but they do know that they seldom need specific advice, an instruction telling them what to do. They do need to know how to achieve a given strategy at a given cost and what to do if the strategy is not effective. Information that certain physicians' care profiles exceed the average is only useful if it can help to change a behavior pattern. Similarly, showing hospital departments comparative figures to motivate them to coordinate staffing patterns may not work. Information fails to take into consideration the power relationship of organizaitonal components to provide action strategies within organizational constraints.

Managers learn through experience to make use of multiple informtion systems to permit the greatest possible room for strategy creation. Mangers often make use of an information system based on relationships within the organization, to supplement both the informal and formal information systems.

4. The Problem of the Separation of Organizational Life and Information Systems. Objectives in organizations are multiple, conflicting, and vague. Objectives for data conversion need to be single, sequential, and precise, because it is not possible to maximize opposing elements simultaneously. The question of what objectives to pursue becomes less precise as information moves to the top of the organization, where defining the problem to be resolved within operational resources and constraints may come late in the decision-making process, or where available action strategies may not, if fact, relate to optimal ("informed") choice. Information on preferred strategies or relationships among constraints may be more useful but are more difficult to come by. Information systems assume that decisions are made prospectively, but organizations may need information to rationalize decisions retrospectively. The distinctions among management levels and constraints become more complex and less understood as one moves toward the top of the organization (Gorry and Scott Morton, 1971).

Evidence from the study of the hospital organization indicates that managers did not consider MIS- produced data useful, and in fact, the data did not appear to meet their needs, as managers described them. First, department managers were more concerned with monitoring specific program elements, such as budgets, productivity, billing, or staffing. The administrator was primarily concerned with information regarding the impact of the hospital as a whole. For example, how was the hospital being received in the local community? Was it considered a high-quality hospital? Second, managers were most concerned with monitoring those programs or their elements or components over which they could exercise direct control, such as a salary increase for one class of workers as opposed to another class. The administrator was likely to be interested in outcomes that were products of variables in addition to program impact, such as the cumulative effect of new wage packages upon the hospital's budgets over the next two or three years.

The reason managerial needs were poorly met has to do with the structure of the MIS. The managerial perspective is one that attempts to identify the most important variables in a program and the most important casual relationships among those variables, as well as the options within the manager's control which, when applied to the variables in question, will achieve the desired results. Managers are searching for an understanding of relationships within their particular programs, and wish to identify important points where their interaction will have maximum impact. What managers want is a model of their *own* programs as systems made of elements and strategies tied to each other in a structure of causal relationships: If you do this at this point, you will get this result.

TABLE 4   What Information Do Managers and Administrators Need?

	WHAT DATA ARE IMPORTANT?	
	Managers	Administrators (senior managers)
They do:	manage specific programs	manage total organization
They need to know:	important relationships; options for action	what impact of organization is
They are interested in:	significant variables; important relationships among variables	outcomes, quality of end product; products of many variables together
They look for:	direct image of specific programs	long-range impact of all programs

On the other hand, the administrator tends to monitor variables that are beyond the control of lower managers. The administrator looks to the long-range impact of program policies rather than to the direct impacts of individual units or programs. Data needed by the administrator must basically fulfill the criteria for evaluation. That is, data must be aggregated and compared across programs. If we compare the functions of the administrator in terms of models and systems the administrator monitors general inputs into the system, and general outputs. He or she evaluates the system based loosely upon input-output comparisons (Is what is coming out worth what is going in?). However, the administrator does not usually monitor variables and relationships among variables within specific units or programs, or usually distinguish among the various causes of an output. Individual program effectiveness or unit productivity may be only one of several factors contributing to an end product that is the basis for evaluation. The end product, moreover, may be only loosely defined as a desired level of quality, service, or income.

The implications of this perspective are that information directed to program or unit managers is more likely to be used if it is based on models of the programs in question, if it is directed to problems plausibly within the control of managers, and if it is designed to include data that are soft, or at least less than ideally suited to manipulation by computer, but which, nonetheless, give clues to the causal relations of elements within programs (Emery, 1967).

If data are shifted to reflect the givens and the variables managers need and to be more useful to them, they will be shifted further away from the needs of policy makers at higher levels, who are concerned with such questions as, "Are the organization's goals being achieved by given strategies?" "Are there new qualities that should be aimed at?" A second implication is that management decision-making depends on a feedback process to modify what administrators do in a continuous process of search and adjustment of means to ends, ends to means, and so forth. To achieve a good fit requires that analysis be substituted for the inadequacy of information. Analysis becomes one of several constraints to which the administrator is subject, as well as the primary strategy for dealing with uncertainty at the level of the organization (Wildavsky, 1974).

NOTE

1. For the classic discussion of organizational levels, see Simon, 1960.

7

Typologies of Information and Organization

"INFORMATION," AS WILDAVSKY writes, "is an organizational problem," in that the primary task of organizational structure — units, levels, hierarchies — is to screen data sufficiently so that only meaningful, manipulative parts remain (Wildavsky and Yurow, 1979). MIS have, for the most part, performed adequately at lower levels of the organization, processing large volumes of data with purposefulness, as long as singularity of objectives and clarity of calculation exist. As objectives become multiple and calculation uncertain, however, there is less probability that the data derived will be both meaningful and sufficiently reduced in quantity to be useful. This is necessarily true because the main function of organization is to divide the world into meaningful units for purposes of control. An information system should not increase data flow, for a major problem with proliferating data is that it increases error and decreases learning from error. Furthermore, the information system designed to serve everyone ends up serving few, since it is impossible to maximize every goal simultaneously. This approach not only violates some important aspects of problem-solving, but it ignores some vital aspects of organizational structure as well. It is important to understand these aspects in order to deal more effectively with complexity.

GENERALITY AND POWER

Although *generality* and *power* (Newell, 1969) have different meanings in different contexts, a specific definition of these terms is intended here. Generality is defined as the "number" aspect of a solution (and what is a decision but a solution to a particular problem?). Generality indicates the scope of a solution, that is, the number of problems undertaken simultaneously or the number of problems that can be handled by the same solution. Generality may be measured differently in different domains. For example, one may attempt to solve all urban ills or one can attempt to solve all health-related urban ills. Although one of these attempts is less general than the other, both are still considered general strategies, because no clearly defined, mutually agreed-upon goal is articulated.

Power is the "size" quality of the solution, the degree of fit or explanation achieved by a solution. A perfect fit requires the ability to explain and to predict all aspects of the problem domain undertaken. A cure for a particular disease may be a powerful solution, since almost all agree upon its problem area (the disease) and the cure works most of the time for most instances of the specific problem. However, the cure will not work if it is applied to another domain of problem. For the most part, only in situations of near-perfect knowledge can one have both general and powerful solutions, and even in these cases, the problem domain is usually defined rather narrowly. Thus, general and powerful solutions are usually limited to purely technical problems, since there is not sufficient information on the behavior of human beings and their organizations to allow for general, powerful solutions. As Rittel and Webber (1973) have pointed out, social problems are so "wicked" that even when one thinks one has solved them, there are usually many unresolved difficulties.

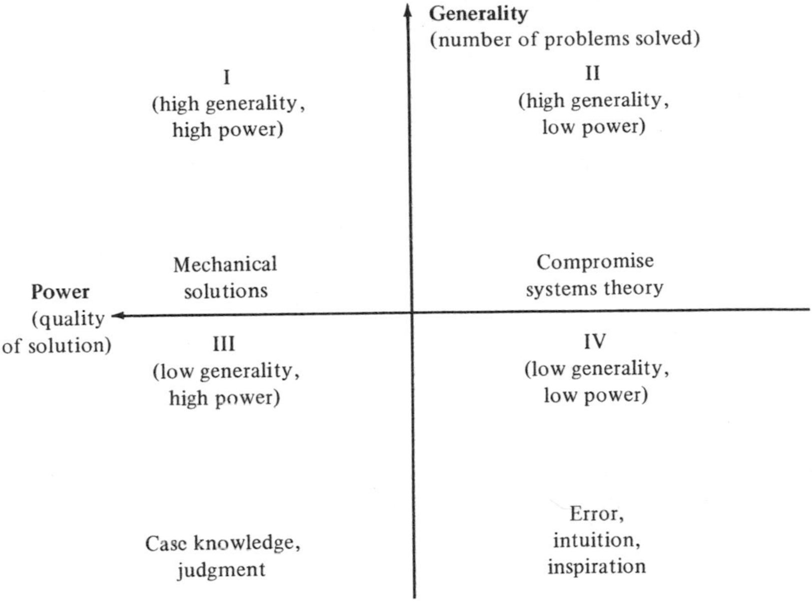

FIGURE 1

The matrix in Figure 1 may help to clarify the two qualities. In the first quadrant, both generality and power are very high. Thus, perfect knowledge of the entire problem is required. Such perfect knowledge is usually found only in mechanical systems, where all aspects of the system are thoroughly understood (since they are human creations). Many decisions are often erroneously assigned to this quadrant because of the assumption that sufficient information for such an assignation exists.

The second quadrant is characterized by high generality and low power. Compromise decisions belong in this quadrant because they attempt to cover all relevant situations, with offense to no individual party. Despite the attempts of general-systems-theory advocates to place their solutions in the first quadrant, these solutions more often belong in the area of high generality/low power. Lacking real information about human behavior, systems theorists attempt to cover all aspects of a decision. In this they cannot succeed, which leads to the necessity for such weak solutions.

The third quadrant is one into which many decisions may be placed. Decisions in this quadrant have the characteristics of low generality and high power; they are usually instances of case-by-case knowledge or individual judgement. Understanding of all aspects relevant to the particular situation may be lacking, but a solution that covers and solves the problem and one that will work in any other case of the same problem can be found by those two methods.

Decisions characterized by low generality and low power are assigned to the fourth quadrant. Obviously, erroneous decisions are marked by these qualities, but decisions made by inspiration or intuition are also well described. They characterize the so-called stroke of genius.

IMPLICATIONS OF THE
GENERALITY/POWER TYPOLOGY

The matrix of this typology illustrates a classic dilemma: One usually cannot have both power and generality built into one's solutions. For almost all cases, one is either satisfied with weak solutions of high generality and low power or with case or judgmental solutions of high power and low generality. This relationship can also be expressed as a function, graphed in Figure 2.

Allen Newell (1969) has indicated that the tradeoff between generality and power is implicitly recognized by the general problem solver, who seeks ever weaker solutions to a difficult, broadly defined problem. As one increases the generality of one's hypothesis, the ability to derive powerful solutions proportionately decreases. Newell's formulation of the tradeoff is a hypothetical one, designed to serve as a guide to the design of heuristic programs, but other authors have also recognized the tradeoff in more concrete situations.

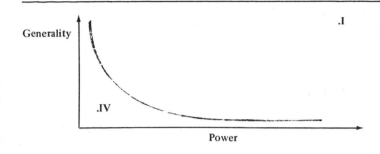

FIGURE 2

James C. Emery (1967) took explicit notice of the costs of different systems attributes. Emery identified six factors important for information cost: volume, selectivity of output, response time, accuracy and reliability, generality, and flexibility. Some of these factors are associated with machine characteristics (i.e., machine response time and volume), but others are suggestive to the person interested in solution-cost relationships. Emery indicates, for example, that periodic, general-purpose reports are cheap, but that the attempt to handle exceptions (to introduce power) into these reports is costly. Emery also realizes that a general system (one with many "design features," in his language) is expensive in lost efficiency. It is therefore concluded that a balance between value and cost exists — another way of indicating the inverse relationship between system requirements.

Danziger (n.d.) posited hidden costs. He believed that many EDP systems only exist at the cost of other organizational features, which do not appear in cost-accounting reports. Management information systems, designed to be general, lead to a significant loss of organizational power. For example, local government EDP systems stimulate data overcollection, diluting the attention any one problem may be given and diverting resources from more effective endeavors. Daniziger also noted that EDP systems are insensitive to the quantative aspects of performance, indicating that, once again, the desire for general information applicable to every member of an organization is costly in terms of the ability to understand the activities of any one actor.

Information for policy decision requires data collected according to some scheme that says," If you do this, you will get this result." The scheme has to have in it variables that can be manipulated by the person to whom this information is addressed, at the level of the organization that person occupies. It is important to consider these requirements because data storage, collection, updating, and filtering are functions of the size of the data base. If an organization's resources are limited, the more data are collected, the fewer resources (time, money, energy) will be available for other uses.

UNCERTAINTY AND RISK

A complementary view of problem-solving related to generality and power treats uncertainty and risk as critical factors in decision-making. The only conduct amendable to control is the future, yet to every choice for future conduct is attached a liability. Analysis requires judgement and evaluation to determine the magnitude of this liability. We draw a distinction between a measurable uncertainty (a risk) and an unmeasurable one (whose risk is unknown). The term *risk* is ordinarily used in a general way to refer to any kind of uncertainty viewed from the standpoint of the unfavorable contingency. The term *uncertainty,* similarly, is used with reference to the favorable outcome (Knight, 1964). In this way, we speak of a business risk or the uncertainty of gain.

The practical difference between the two categories, risk and uncertainty, is that in the former, the distribution of the outcome in a group of instances is known through theoretical calculation, or from a statistical distribution, while in the case of uncertainty, the distribution is unknown. The existence of a predictive theory provides a priori probability, for it ensures homogeneous classification of instances that are identical, so that problem-solving can proceed logically.

Statistical probability is an evaluation of the frequency of association between variables not classifiable into varying combinations of equally probable alternatives. In this instance, however, it is not possible to eliminate all factors not really indeterminate. It is just as impossible to enumerate the equally probable alternatives involved and to determine their mode of combination, so as to increase the probability of a calculation. The statistical category rests on an empirical classification to form a group of instances, for since situations are unique, they do not aggregate sufficient experience to permit statistical analysis. In terms of administrative or organizational, but not medical, decision-making, cast in an organizational perspective, the higher up the organizational hierarchy a decision resides, the more likely it is to rest on uncertainty about both the consequences of alternatives and the probability of their occurring. There are a number of reasons this should be true: the largeness of decisions, the interconnectedness, the difficulties of problems, the greater number of objectives, the far greater known as well as unknown consequences of relationships. One reason the hospital via its board of trustees retains control over medical staff appointments is that there is enormous uncertainty in medical practice and a great risk of malpractice.

Considering the effects of a particular course of action and the probabilities that the effects will in fact occur, gives several possible outcomes (See Figure 3). Under conditions of risk, we can predict with reasonable certainty what outcomes will obtain. Chance is a condition where it is possible to know the outcome will happen, but not to know exactly what the outcome will be (e.g., to know that a major contributor will probably decrease contribution to the hospital, but not to know by how much). Cell 4 describes a condition of ignorance, in that a decision must be made where neither the effects nor the probability of the outcomes occurring is known, due to the uncertain nature of real estate. Cell 3 describes a decision situation where

	Effects		
	Known	Not known	
Effects known Probabilities known	+ + 1	+ − 2	Effects unknown Probabilities known
Effects known Probabilities unknown	3 − +	4 − −	Effects unknown Probabilities unknown

Outcomes:

Cell 1	Effects known Probability known	Risk (theory)
Cell 2	Effects not known Probability known	Chance
Cell 3	Effects known Probability not known	Uncertainty
Cell 4	Effects unknown Probability unknown	Ignorance

FIGURE 3

we may know the effects but not be capable of specifying with any reliability the probability of their occurring. A 20 percent increase in Medicare /Medicaid patients will, we know, impact upon the hospital, but we do not know if there will in fact be a 20 percent increase.

Organizations would not survive in a state of ignorance, but risk, chance, and uncertainty occur in all organizations to one degree or another. Indeed, we employ a classic paradigm to denote this, indicating that whoever sits at the top of an organization has the "riskiest" job of all, being faced, for the most part, with the highest amount of chance and uncertainty the organization endures, since at this level problems generally present themselves in such a complicated way that either knowledge or agreement on objectives is incomplete. We say that judgment, experience, and intuition are effective skills to employ at this level. In other words, administrators themselves should be "general problem-solving systems."

THE PROBLEM OF "RATIONALITY"

The rational organization is interested in increasing effectiveness and productivity and in eliminating irrational responses that impair productivity. But how does the desire to act rationally become organizational action? The usual paradigm of rationality calls for searching out independent variables or change agents, then moving either incrementally or synoptically to eliminate whatever is causing the trouble. Rationality, as Landau (1969) views it, is prescriptive: "Given a condition which is deemed unsatisfactory, and a condition which constitutes a desirable solution, find the set of operations (the instruments, processes, organizations, institutions) that will produce the preferred state." But Landau immediately warns that the production of a desirable outcome is "no easy task." While we assume that once the perceptions of members are engaged actions will proceed accordingly, there is little evidence to support this assumption.

First, behavioral linkages beween action and belief often lack adequate description. We know from the behavioral psychologists that, at least on an individual level, perceiving a need for action and wanting to act may not be sufficient conditions for action to occur. Once we assume that organizations are collections of individual as well as interacting behaviors, the task of linking perception with action becomes enormously more difficult because of the scale and complexity involved.

Second, knowledge, in terms of a theory or, at the very minimum, a correct description of the condition to be acted upon, is not so easy to come by. Landau (1969) reports that "inadequate description obscures the prevailing codes and renders it difficult to locate or identify those linkage points which might be profitably exploited." What Landau implies is that failure to produce success is "as much a result of inadequate initial state description as it is [of] inferior praxiology."

Weick (1969) notes that task analysis has been neglected in part because there is an insufficient number of taxonomies for describing tasks. The more complex something is, the less described it is. However, Weick warns that even if tasks are specified sufficiently, "there still remains the problem of specifying the precise ways in which acceptance is translated into a given amount of effort and into accomplishment of the task." Weick (1969: 40) suggests one reason attempts to describe the relationship between belief and action have not been successful is that cognition may have "little effect on behavior because it follows rather than precedes behavior":

> Cognitions may be retrospective; they may make sense of what has happened rather than what will happen. Plans for the future may have little control over behavior because they are basically content-free. It is actions that provide the content for cognitions, and in the absence of action, congitions are vacuous.

Weick's point is that the function of cognition may be to summarize and interpret action that has already occured, to "encode it" as Landau would say, rather than to predict future activity.

WHY ARE PREFERRED OUTCOMES PROBLEMATIC?

> While we are often able to provide a clear description of what is to be attained, as problems grow more complicated, we find it increasingly difficult to clarify our goals [so] as to enable the measurement of achievement. Then, too, goal states are frequently the object of bitter controversy [Landau, 1969].

A part of the problem of joining perception to action is in designating where to move and what to prefer, for efforts to establish preferences over outcomes may require such explicitness that they inevitably "do violence to organizational reality by emphasizing certain activities (and hence organizational

Values

		+		−	
+	1	Programmatic		2 Bargaining	
Facts					
−	3	Incremental		4 Anomic	

FIGURE 4

elements) over others. Thus the very process of defining objectives may be considered a hostile act."

> If they are too vague, no evaluation can be done. If they are too specific, they never encompass all the indefinable qualities that their adherents insist they have [Landau, 1969].

There is an overwhelming tendency in organizations to assume that the organization contains sufficient information in and of itself to resolve problems, and to attempt to build a MIS that embodies this belief. This view overlooks, however, the organizational dichotomy of the authority of value premises (the structure) and the authority of factual premises (function).

ORGANIZATIONAL DECISION-MAKING

The discrepency between values and facts disappears when they are placed in a means-end chain, because these premises become transformed into instruments with causal properties, which provides the subclassification of decision-making in Figure 4 (Landau, 1969).

OUTCOMES

Cell 1: Programmatic. When factual knowledge is complete and values are in agreement, decision makers can proceed on the basis of a closed set of variables. Knowledge is deterministic and decision is computational, in that only a signal is required to set into motion a predictable and highly certain outcome.

Cell 2: Incremental. Here preferences are known, but how to achieve them is not. The important questions turn around matters of fact, so that decisions must be made in the face of contingency, on experimental-pragmatic considerations. Certainty has vanished because knowledge is weak.

Cell 3: Bargaining. Here there is no question about facts; what there is to know is known, but the question concerns divisions over preferences. Decision requires the bargaining out of differences and proceeds primarily by means of compromise and agreement.

Cell 4: Anomie. Here neither knowledge nor preference exists. No decision is entailed as anomie sets in.

Most organizations construe themselves as if they existed in environments characterized by cell 1 (perfect rationality), and try to construct management information systems specialized to this purpose. In reality, very little of organizational life falls into cell 1; instead it falls into cell 2 or cell 3, where either the necessary factual premises or sufficient value agreement is missing. Therefore, the MIS is frequently deficient in informing management decision-making. The hospital, for example, had only very limited areas of activity where decisions could proceed computationally; primarily these are at the operations level. Questions of development and planning for the future, for example, must proceed on the basis either that new resources will be acquired to match existing preferences or that new preferences will be acquired to match existing resources. Any action taken must be submitted to revision, through either the acquistion of new knowledge or the imposition of new values. When past values changed, the hospital added new sets of services: the podiatry clinic and an array of functions directed to the older population. When new facts became available, services were eliminated: the obstetrics unit. Even when a factual basis is strong enough to permit adequate solution, a mechanism such as bargaining may still be necessary to sequentially process remaining problems, such as whether or not to decrease or increase a department's budget. Bargaining can provide a basis for the creation of new knowledge in the organization.

Analysis must act to overcome the deficiencies of knowledge by attempting continuously to reformulate direction through an understanding and an evaluation of organizational function. Since better information alone will not matter without incentives for organizations to use it, analysis must deal with incentives. At the same time, knowing what is wrong without knowing what to do about it means that there can be no possiblity of intelligent action or improvement; thus, information has to be capable of conveying desirable new alternatives to managers; the task of analysis is to bring about a resolution of missing facts or insufficient value accord by supplying new premises for organized action. Should this resolution not occur, then the organization will fall into cell 4, anomie.

Centralizing data and shooting them to the top of the managerial hierarchy will usually be counter-productive: It will probably not answer the questions of the administrator and will simply add to the overload of data he or she processes. Detailed data do not tell the administrator how to proceed when uncertainty over preferences, facts, or their interrelationship exists. There are such questions as, Will the increasing propensity of doctors to utilize the five-hour surgery unit create unwanted secondary or tertiary effects on other units, which will actually offset gains the five-hour ward might make? How can certain doctors be convinced that their definition of "short-stay" surgery is stretching the hospital's definition? Should service X rather than service or unit Y be added, on the basis of a predicted demand over the next decade, or is it possible that new information will be developed after the organization has undertaken a costly commitment to the project? If technological equipment ABG is purchased at a heavy sink cost, will its doctor backers still be enthusiastic about it a year from now?

A hospital is a complex system. Organizations are enabled to survive complexity by reducing it into concepts that can be adequately encompassed within conceptual codes and decision rules to produce regular and predictable responses to uncertainty. What does complexity mean? In Herbert Simon's words (1969), complexity is

> made up of a large number of parts that interact in a non-simple way. In such systems the whole is more than the sum of the parts, not in an ultimate metaphysical sense, but in the important pragmatic sense that given the properties of the parts and the laws of interaction, it is not a trivial matter to infer the properties of the whole.

COMPLEXITY AS PROBLEM

Reducing complexity to manageable proportions means that certain aspects of complexity must be taken into consideration. These aspects are that (1) complexity is generally hierarchically organized and composed of smaller parts or subsystems; (2) there is a relationship between the structure of a complex system and the time required for it to evolve from a simple to a more complex organization; (3) problem-solving involves trial-and-error searches that are feedback-dependent; and (4) in a complex, hierarchically organized system, interactions at one level are generally different from those at another level.

The important point that Simon (1969) makes about complexity is its decomposability. Decomposable elements, like building blocks, can be grafted onto an organization or severed with relative ease as well as cause little disturbance either to other blocks or to the whole organization. Simon argues that the most attractive feature is that most complex systems can be decomposed into stable subassemblies and that these are the crucial elements in any organization or system.

Decomposability draws attention to the element of coupling: A System can be broken down and reconstructed, once a simple linkage of elements becomes stable. Over time it is more likely to be capable of expansion into a more complex assembly (new knowledge is once more incorporated into the assembly). If problem-solving is by trial and error and feedback-dependent, then small, stable linkages will generate more knowledge than large unstable (nonhierarchical) ones, because feedback time is reduced. If elements can be broken down into subassemblies, then so can the information the subassemblies need, so it is not necessary to collect and store all the system's data — just those that are relevant to the linked components.

HOW THE HOSPITAL DEALT WITH COMPLEXITY

For an overview of the hospital's MIS and complexity, see Table 5.

The MIS made an already complex environment and collection of behaviors even more complex. It did this because the hospital failed to think about how it could transform its complex financial system in the most efficient and effective manner.

1. It opted to attempt to serve the entire financial and accounting system, despite the fact that the system included activities from billing to development and planning, activities which were carried out on different organizational levels, and, because of considerable differences in scope, recency of data, degree of aggregation, time frames, and so forth, did not really have very much in common. These activities, moreover, were ideally suited for severing with little disturbance to the total system.

2. It chose to try to serve the entire system at one shot, and maximize simultaneously on all dimensions, as well as achieve economy of scale by adding more purposes and objectives. In

TABLE 5 The Hospital's MIS and Complexity

Principle of Complexity	Prescription	The Hospital
1. Complex systems often take the form of hierarchy; there are elements within elements	Break the system down into its subassemblies	Tried to replicate the whole system of financial accounting and control
2. The time it takes for simple elements to evolve into complex ones depends on the number and distribution of stable intermediate forms; building blocks or components are the clues to rapid expansion	Think of the subassemblies as components or even "colonies"; link together those that have been "mapped" into larger and larger "mapped" (or agreed-upon) linkages	Tried to link the whole thing together, despite the absence of knowledge of complete mapping of any of the components, or agreement on values
3. Problem-solving is trial-and-error (experience or heuristics), dependent on feedback and "recoding" redundancy into action patents	Pay attention to redundancy, for it builds knowledge by building patents	Tried to eliminate redundancy as "inefficient"
4. Interactions within subassemblies are for the most part independent of interactions among subassemblies; these interaction possibilities require information of different magnitude	Subassemblies, if they are decomposed, need only the information pertinent to their own territories	Did not sufficiently decompose, into subassemblies to facilitate data collection, storage and distribution; stuck with trying to give the entire system everything

reality, since the activities of each element, unit, or component were not completely known, as the system went into operation, new data had to be added because of new discoveries. Then, as these changes were incorporated, conflicts among priorities arose and still more data had to be added. The larger the model grew, the more expensive it became and the less capable of learning from feedback.

3. Because users were highly specialized and differentiated, and because redundancy was not properly understood or was looked upon as an evil, there were an insufficient number of duplicate or overlapping channels. Thus, errors were not discovered and little learning occurred because of insufficient feedback. Patents for behavior, patterns or examples, cannot be developed in the absence of redundancy.

4. Since the system had not been properly decomposed and since feedback and redundancy were not sufficiently developed to foster learning, not only was it impossible to know the relevant intracomponent data necessary to proper functioning, but the system was forced to proliferate the same data system-wide.

Failure to resolve the general principles of complexity made for a MIS that was wasteful of organizational resources and had limited utility to managers. Furthermore, the MIS added complexity to the complexity users already had to cope with. It added complexity in the form of error, procedural complicatedness, and the additional effort needed to get, verify, "underwrite," or test needed data through other channels. It added complexity in that it increased the stress users had to work under.

COMPLEXITY AND ORGANIZATIONAL BEHAVIOR

When data are general but not specific, they are not relevant to the functions and decisions facing managers. When they are inaccessible, late, or do not contain policy-relevant variables, they speak to the power position of managers. A major cause is failures in decomposition. *Complexity requires decomposition of elements into smaller, self-contained units.* Simon's studies support the thesis that the characteristics of human problem-solving and rational choice define the organization's structure and function. People solve problems by simplifying both information search and processing, by attending to a limited number of problem dimensions, and by making decisions on the basis of sufficient knowledge. "The real situation is almost always far too complex to be handled in detail." Since individuals can attend to only a limited number of things at a time. "Rational behavior involves substituting for the complex reality a model of reality that is sufficiently simple to be handled by problem-solving processes." Human intolerance calls for simple strategies and models as problem-solving devices or standard operating tools for satisfying rather than optimizing behavior, while organizational control calls for fragmentation of task by purpose or function (Simon, 1969).

For example, billers grew increasingly mistrustful of the system's complicatedness, especially as they learned that the more complicated things got, the more errors increased, decreasing the billers' ability to exert control over the future. Reluctant to trust the computer's output, they resurrected the old system, the old way of doing things, or old procedures. When problems arose, a popular technique was to look through the files for past examples as a comparison or to ask others if they had experienced similar problems. Billers also changed work schedules and processed whatever was easiest and least problematic, setting aside until last what was most problematic. In general, when the work of production required a smaller effort of time and attention, it was more likely to be completed, not just by the billers, but by all the producing departments as well.

Not only do individuals focus on *limited numbers* of problems by using a fairly standard repertoire of tools, but also the nature of organizational structure assigns people to tasks that are highly fragmented by purpose of function. These functions, in turn, reinforce the kinds of goals people choose to follow. In short, people deal with *limited aspects* of problems. Generally speaking, these decisions are taken on the basis of localized disturbances (Simon, 1957).

The hospital's decision to implement a MIS to serve the entire financial accounting system was contrary to a basic requirement of complexity, as well as to the ways individuals solve problems. The same data base was supposed to relate to systemwide problems, yet problems were not necessarily systemwide; they were localized in specific subunits. The result was that data did not aid decision-making because they bore no resemblance to either the objectives individuals were fostering or the tools with which they were pursuing solutions. Inevitably, data would fit some unit's needs but be all wrong for others. If the billers got detailed data, those data were not suitable for the board. If the administrator got trends and graphs, they were not of much use to anyone else.

EVOLUTION OF COMPLEXITY

The more data were added to the system to cope with user needs, the more difficult and costly models were to change and the harder they were to control. Inappropriate data got to people who could not use them, such as the billing summaries sent to the administrator, who really wanted trend analyses. At the same time, the harder things were to control, the harder they were to change, because organizational change requires both knowledge and power. The purpose of error is to encourage reexamination of new premises through knowledge-building, and thereby build the conditions for change by communicating desirable alternatives to managers who may not always welcome the prospect of change, since they may prefer the stability and the promotion of existing activities instead. Department managers actively resisted changing to new budgetary procedures and new charge forms or schedules. They were used to working with, and getting around, the systems they already knew. The introduction of new ones would require an investment of time and effort, and they had no guarantee that they would, in fact, get anything out of their efforts.

Change requires not just the will to act, but a basis in fact as well, for it is only when information is provided to the level that can and will use it, within the constraints of the resources available to it, that change can occur. When the scope of the model is large, error may not be easily visible and may not be evaluated so that it becomes possible to learn from experience or design. When models are broad in scope, each additional component introduces less that is known than is not known, because the state of knowledge of structure, which is already weak, becomes weaker still when it is added to the whole and must interact with still other components. Permitting interaction does not necessarily mean that anyone has control over it or that any learning takes place. Furthermore, each addition of demand, objective, or need constrains the model even more. When ratio reports were developed for some managerial functions, which wanted merely a summary comparison of the hospital, these reports caused misery to other management functions, which needed dollar reports in order to compare their own standing. Yet dollar reports, in turn, were not useful to still other groups, whose objective was to process quantities or days in revenue.

Proceeding with change requires agreement on facts as well as on values. People must agree that the facts available adequately describe a situation they have to work with, and unless the simple is attacked first and built upon as a basis for the more complicated or conflicting, the organization does not have a basis for action; error and resistance will be expensive and time-consuming. Rather than start with comprehensive, multipurpose models, it is better to start with smaller processes and build up as agreement and learning are realized by those who have to live with the results.

CONCLUSION

AFTER LONG AND THOUGHTFUL consultation, a MIS is installed. Yet nothing planned works, except low-level and routine transactions, or what is planned works with difficulty, after many and time-consuming adaptations are effected. As time passes, it becomes increasingly clear that if the higher functions of the system are to be implemented — functions that will aid in forecasting service demand and hospital utilization, and analyzing and planning development — they can only be achieved by major adaptations requiring considerable funds and time. Furthermore, it is by no means certain that change in software or hardware will actually result in the creation of either effective or efficient programs capable of improving decisions at upper managerial levels. The organization then has the choice of proceeding as it is, and processing routine work through an expensive MIS that is now really nothing more than a data-processing system, or attempting to recoup its original investment in a MIS by plowing in additional funds, without any guarantee that it will in fact be any further down the road at the end.

A PROGRESS RECORD

The hospital's objectives in instituting this system were revenue capture and cost containment. The system was envisioned as simple and straightforward: producing budgets and special reports on one hand, while on the other, completing Medicare reports and financial statements yet still providing the detailed data base necessary for accurate, timely, day-to-day billing. In undertaking the conversion from a manual and relatively nonstandardized system to a fully automated computer-based MIS, the hospital was stimulated by the effects over time of increasing account-handling costs, as well as by the potential loss of revenue posed by a lengthy turnaround cycle. The old system was limited and labor-intensive, and much of the reporting and financial planning function had to be completed by managers and independent consultants. The hospital wanted to not only to cut the costs of fiscal management, but to achieve better control by reestablishing and centralizing all financial functions within its own organization. If the organization was to expand and develop, it would need careful analysis of its requirements, particularly in light of the highly competitive market, the rising costs of labor and technology, and stringent regulation by planning authorities.

The short-term objectives of the hospital were to increase the cash flow, decrease losses from late and lost charges, develop budget sensitivity on the part of the department managers, and provide management with sensible monitoring and control devices. At the end of a year and a half, however, the following was the result:

A. The new system had disrupted the organization.
   1. People had been fired, or else had resigned over the system.
   2. The original technical staff had left.
   3. Financial services had gone through three different managers.
   4. Most of financial management and control was shifted to a higher managerial level because of excessive error rates.
   5. More outside consultants had to be hired to complete necessary reports.

B. The new system was inefficient.

1. The MIS was running in a continuous state of backlog.

2. Turnabout time on accounts had decreased by only a few days.

3. Additional staff had been permanently added to the department.

4. Operating statements were still being issued months in arrears, and the budget process was indefinitely delayed.

5. Incomplete records were still backlogged.

C. The new system was ineffective.

1. Management reports were completed manually or orally, because the system could not develop trending and survey capacity.

2. Overtime on the system was running high.

3. A number of reports were being hand-compiled off other reports, or had simply been delayed indefinitely.

4. Error rates were high.

5. Absenteeism and stress were high.

6. Employee turnover was at its highest point in history.

It was also clear that thousands of dollars in additonal modifications to the MIS would be required to fulfill original objectives.

THE HOSPITAL'S INTENTIONS

What the hospital wanted to achieve with a MIS was to get data to managers who made financial decisions — the right data in the right format at the right time. Managers of departments wanted data on budget performance: How well was their department conforming with the budget? Where was there slack? Where would there be trouble? Departments needed data in order to relate effort to performance. Were they processing a load sufficient to justify the present technician hours? Would automating some processes by justified? What percentage of time was devoted to purely clerical matters? Other managers, of purchasing and personnel, for example, needed data that aggregated hospital income for particular time frames so that they would know how to make the most efficient use of their funds. Without hard data on income and expense, it would be difficult to know what recommendations to make about capital-intensive purchases, or whether or not the hospital should acquire scarce but expensive technical expetise at this time. Administration and the board of directors wanted to know about performance comparisons, where the hospital stood on its financial obligations, and what income could be deployed most successfully for what purposes.

Under the old, inefficient system, each unit worked independently of the others, made its own rules, and set its own priorities. The formal information channel transmitted patient information almost exclusively, relegating almost all other information relevant to running the hospital to the informal network, where intermediaries in the form of levels, interest groups, and strategic elites actually functioned to prevent too much information from overloading the organizational levels. In the old system there was duplication and redundancy, but the overlap reduced the need for coordination among all the units. As long as self-interest and self-reliance were synchronized, each unit could attend to its own "local rationality," and error-control systems could function smoothly. In this way the top of the organization was freed to manage change and adaptation to new circumstances, and control, or pace, the spread of innovation. All this changed with the bigger, more efficient MIS. The publicness of the system revealed differences in budgets, in personnel evaluation or operating agreements which had previously been negotiated one-on-one. Department energies were deflected into competition with other departments, status differences were magnified. With each unit responsible for a specific portion of the new general-purpose form, sequence and timing requirements were stringent. Status differences were exacerbated, however, because the financial units were unable to coerce the medical units into sacrificing patient care for paper-pushing.

The hospital assumed that financial accounting and control were simple and straightforward, and that data could therefore be readily supplied to all users at all levels, regardless of functional disparity and different objectives. It also assumed that even if knowledge and agreement over tasks were incomplete, it would be possible to serve everyone. Further, it assumed that eliminating redundancy and increasing differentiation would maximize utility as well as the hospital's investment of resources and effort. The result was data that did not relate to user needs and that introduced conflict, could not encompass change, and could not be controlled with ease (See Table 6).

The purpose of an information system is to substitute order and simplicity for the complexity and chaos in the real world. Information systems do this by abstracting the essential features of complex realities into simpler laws, by taking in data in

TABLE 6   Responses to Complexity

ASPECTS OF COMPLEXITY		FAILURE TO RESOLVE	
Of behavior	*Of environment*	*Results in*	*Causing*
Objectives are multiple, conflicting, and vague	Structure moves from simple (less uncertain) to complex (uncertain)	Overreduction	Data low in quality
Reduction of variety is necessary to combat uncertainty	Management levels are information-specific	Overcollection	Variety that is not reduced
Evaluation proceeds by learning and agreeing	Learning needs feedback	Overdistribution	Data that do not aid decision-making
People and organization are constrained	Complexity can be decomposed, uncoupled	Interconnection	Error difficult to control

one form and translating them into alternative forms, while all
the time searching for methods to map the new and changing
phenomena into familiar codes. If organizations did not do this,
they would in time be overwhelmed, yet it is very difficult to
match the organization's variety with sufficient variety to enable the MIS to successfully regulate the organization. Even
when subunits of a system are individually understood, when
they are all linked together into a larger system, the new larger
system may require a different order of explanation.

The hospital failed to resolve the complexity of the task-
and/or problem-solving it should have tackled at the start. It
built a system that fused and linked units, and by attempting to
maximize simultaneously and make all the data good for all the
parts, it eliminated redundancy and increased the potential of
error to disrupt the organization.

The match between an organization's environmental complexity and its set of adaptive responses in large part determines
its survival. The ability to reduce the complexity and variety of
the environment to adequate rules of solution in large part
determines the success of the MIS. There is little point in
having a MIS if it increases the burden of complexity for the
organization's problem solvers.

The hospital ended up with a MIS that was infinitely less
reliable than any of its parts, for it lacked integrity. The attempt
to reduce all purposes and objectives to one or two general ones
meant that no one really got what was needed, and all were
served poorly. Since the subunits used ostensibly the same data
for different functions, the system was highly susceptible to the
importation of error, for what might be error might not necessarily look like error to users looking at the data for different
purposes. Interrelating the subunits caused error permeability,
for disasters in one part of the system could not be kept from
invading other parts, resulting in long waits, early closing dates
on overlarge runs, system down-time, reruns, error correction
lists, amendments, and updates. Overdistributing the data
meant that producer and consumer would be separated by
intervening layers of users, so it would be difficult to trace out

error, and it also meant that most users would get only a gross version of what they actually needed and little of the data would be useful to decision-making, because the needs of managers were often contradictory. This was borne out by the attitude of users toward the system, in that they either ignored it, subverted it, or invented alternatives of their own.

DESIGN FAILURES AS FAILURES IN TRADEOFFS

The consequences of the failure to comprehend and organize successfully the complexity in the organization's environment resulted in many problems for the hospital and considerable cost and effort. The hospital failed to make certain tradeoffs. These tradeoffs are basic to an understanding of complexity.

1. Between Generality and Power. The distinction here refers to quality of solution. For the most part in the social domain, there is a tradeoff between generality and power (Newell, 1969): As generality is increased, the ability to derive powerful solutions decreases. To introduce power, however, requires the ability to explain and predict all aspects of the problem domain attacked. Since perfect knowledge is difficult to come by, it is not usually possible to have both power and generality built into solutions. Therefore, as the scope of a model is increased, its utility for subsectors is diminished. In almost all instances, the choice is between weak solutions of high generality and low power, and solutions high in power but low in generality. A MIS designed to be general leads to a loss in organizational power: Attention is diverted, resources are encumbered, and the system is still insensitive to the qualitative aspects of performance and to subsection needs. Because managers need powerful information, a general information system is often distrusted and ignored. Attempts to introduce power, however, are expensive in that the system has relevance to a reduced number of problems, subsections, or users. Further, it is expensive in that introducing exception-type quality has political costs: Users perceive power gains and losses to be a zero-sum game where what one person gains, another loses. Since the chances of data being applicable to all managerial levels is low, the only way to have information solutions that are both general and powerful is to reduce the domain of problems undertaken.

2. *Between Loose and Tight Coupling.* Problem-solving essentially means decomposing problems into their attributes (Simon, 1969). Individuals attend to only a limited number of problem facets at one time, and under pressure of time and circumstances are forced to make decisions with incomplete knowledge of available options, consequences, and probabilistics. Cyert and March (1966) add that if we assume actors have limited rationality, then it follows that decisions will be made in terms of localized disturbances and time constraints. It is not necessary for a decision maker always to know the whole picture, since he or she is rarely going to be making synoptic decisions. Instead, a decision maker needs to know the options available at the *margin,* where a difference will be felt. The choice is between marginal increments of various alternatives and complete pictures. But the picture can never be complete, because without a strong social theory there is no compelling evidence to indicate when completion has been achieved. Therefore, when a system aims to be comprehensive, it often results in being hypercomprehensive; by waiting around for a complete picture and then inundating the decision maker with data, paralysis, rather than action, may result. The performance trends reports for the board of directors were never completed, because reducing all the facts proved to be overwhelming for the system. In reality, however, all the board wanted was a simple statement in graphic form of how well or poorly things were going over a rather short period. The hospital should have opted for much smaller, rather than more general, activity profiles, where a number of users could agree on the important variables and on how much of the action could be accepted as given. The idea is to think microscopically rather than macroscopically. In this way, comprehensiveness, on a reduced scale,

is more easily achieved, and users can devote their attention to what changes, rather than what continues as usual.

Units that have little in common should not be linked because they will not "know the territory" (Weick, 1976) between them well enough to recognize what does not belong there (i.e., error). When units that share a number of characteristics or variables are linked together, they are more likely to be reciprocal. When units are reciprocal, they are dependent on one another and can get each other to comply. In terms of producing and consuming information, this means not only that producer and consumer can describe and contract the terms of their relationship, but also that they can hold one another accountable if they do not get the right data, or if those data are in error. A large system linking every unit does not have this control and in fact generally transfers accountability to the system or its technicians, since producers and consumers are separated and relationships among the linked units (such as billing and planning) may be tenuous. For example, recognizing and agreeing upon the significant variables is a necessary condition for reciprocity. But it is not a *sufficient* condition unless units have the same values regarding the significance and weight of variables, since unless they do so, they will not place the same priority on the data, which means they may not produce data predictably or be willing to bargain out their difficulties satisfactorily if problems arise. Consider the futility of tightly linking medical records and the billing people. Medical records sees itself as part of a medical recording and reporting system, with responsibility for completing a health-related report, or else incurring penalties which could jeopardize the hospital's professional standing. It sees no particular advantage in making the completion of records for the express purpose of billing requirements a number-one priority, for it takes considerable effort to get these records ready for the use of billing, and medical records derives little gain; processing records is an endless activity. Billing, on the other hand, feels medical records should get records prepared for billing, first of all.

Another disadvantage of separating producers and consumers is that the consumer gets little chance to specify what he or she needs, and the producers have no idea why they are producing whatever they are asked to produce. Producers then pass on only what shows their unit in a good light, because they do not know if the data will be used against them. Departments were generally reluctant to report personnel productivity because they feared too good a showing would get part of their budget snatched away, while too poor a performance would invite pressure and destroy a margin of slack vital to their particular working conditions.

3. *Between a Public and a Private Good.* The dilemmas of collective versus individual rationality have been addressed. The problem of public goods is that if individual efforts are likely to be costly and unlikely to change the outcome in a situation, then individuals are likely to abstain from cooperating. In this way what is individually rational results in collective irrationality for the participants (Olson, 1971).

In terms of producing input data, it was clearly in the interests of every unit in the collectivity to produce. However, producing data did not guarantee that the units would get back the operating statements they needed. Therefore, from the individual point of view, compliance might be costly and still not effective, for if a unit produced and the others did not, it would still not get data; yet if everyone produced and it did not, it would probably escape the costs of production altogether, since billing would come and do its work for it. Early in the game the ambulatory care center learned that it could free itself from the costs of producing billing data by not doing the work and then explaining to billing that it had too many medical emergencies to attend to. Billing needed the data very much, so it came and got it itself. The cumulative effects of maximizing on the individual level were costly on the level of the collectivity.

The use of illegal adaptive strategies when output or reports did not meet needs was also individually rational, in that it got a unit or an individual's work done or enabled the unit to fend off disasters. However, when the costs of all the individual adjustments are taken into consideration, they become very expensive, and even then the costs of dislocation and organizational strain cannot be assigned a price. If adaptive strategies are produced or eliminated through system improvements, their costs will still be felt far into the future, because they have been incorporated into the operating premises of the system.

The only way to equalize the distribution of the burden of public goods is to find a way to internalize the rewards and externalize the costs, that is to say, make some of the goods private instead of public by providing incentives or getting units to assume part of the costs of production. In terms of billing, this would mean that producers either produced their share or were penalized or compensated financial services for doing it for them (an in-house service charge). In situations where a monopoly exists, however, pressure to resist this arrangement can be exerted. Doctors, for example, are organized, informed, and constitute a monopoly within the hospital organization. Clearly, other strategies are needed to get doctors to produce completed records for the convenience of the billing system.

4. Between Operational and Strategic Decision-Making. Consider the objectives of the organization: It wants to construct a MIS that will serve the decision-making needs of its management. Management, however, performs different activities: *Stategic planning,* or senior management, is primarily interested in evaluating the opportunities for growth and development in the future. It is involved with the determination of corporate policies and goals and the deployment of resources to meet these goals. *Management control* then takes the strategic plan and divides it into appropriate subdivisions, allocating funds and assigning responsibility for the completion of the plan to persons or groups in the organization. Finally, *operations control* determines the specific mix of people and materials to carry out each portion of the plan. It assigns resources to accomplish the preselected objectives and then compares performance against the planned expectations, and adjusts where necessary.

These are quite standard definitions of managerial levels, primarily derived from the classic work of Robert Anthony. They are ideal types that help conceptualize the integral nature of each level without denying that in practice management requires flexibility and that the divisions between functional levels are never quite so clear-cut as the definitions suggest.

Management activities are quite different at different levels of the organization, so it follows that if the activities performed are different, then the information requirements will also differ sharply among the three areas. Aggregating data from the base is not necessarily useful to those at the other extreme of the organization. When on one occasion the system was able to graph out performance for the use of the board, the detailed data base caused the scale to be so small and the graph so large that the board had difficulty comprehending the significance of deviations. Operations needs large data bases with continuous updating, while strategic planning needs a smaller, more aggregated base.

There are differences in skill requirements at the various management levels. At the level of strategic planning, problems are less structured in presentation, one reason being that the proper question form for the problem to take is unspecified and must be provided. The judgment and insight of the problem solver are primary in question specification. The senior manager is typically his or her own general information system, in that the senior manager's experience, evaluation, and intuition are essential to seeking key relationships. At this level it is important to discriminate between those questions that can be answered and those that cannot. It is necessary to know the relationship of resources to objectives in the system, as well as the relationship of one problem to other key policy areas. The administrator might be interested in knowing how consumer demand five years in the future can be anticipated, so it can be related to the costs of building and of developing political and planning approval, and to public support for the hospital's efforts. On the other hand, the operations manager is an exceptionalist, skilled in a narrow area, working from a problem presented with full (or nearly full) definition. The operations manager's data need primarily to be experimentally derived. He relies on procedural skills rather than judgment and evaluation. The purchasing of supplies or the maintenance and servicing of equipment proceed on the basis of timely, fully derived decision rules. If they have a rule (e.g., whenever stock of a given item falls below a certain point, reorder, or replace various moving parts after a certain number of hours of use), they can proceed as directed, modifying procedures when evidence accumulates to prove an old rule no longer valid.

Now if managers at different levels perform different functions and employ different skills, it follows that they make different kinds of decisions. The basic nature of decisions at the strategic planning level is that they are unique, isolated in time, and often interconnected with a number of other considerations. At the operations level, however, decisions tend to be more like each other because they are more routinized and recurring. As Gorry and Scott Morton (1971) conclude, then, there are few cases where it makes sense to connect management activity directly across boundaries. For example, funneling operations data up to the strategic level makes no sense whatsoever — in fact, if operations data make "sense" at the strategic planning level, the organization has defective management. Yet this was exactly what the hospital was attempting to do by building strategic planning information upon operations-type data. The administrator rarely needs to know the details of any given sector's performance, unless there exists a problem that cannot be resolved or unless a problem threatens the general health of the hospital. He or she merely needs to know that the division of labor is performing in accordance with the delegation of authority. If the administrator does need details on individual performance, it is more likely that the administrator's assistants will acquire special, timely information or make special reports, than that the administrator will personally search through printouts. The more appropriate course of action would be to separate operations from strategic planning. Billing should be fully automated and cast free of fiscal management and financial planning. Those functions, on the other hand, would be better performed by human specialists.

MIS is an internal response to the problems of complexity, yet seldom do organizations ask, before they undertake a MIS, what complexity is, and how the organization is complex. As a consequence, a MIS may not deal adequately with complexity, and in many cases it may even make life more complex for the organization. The costs of dealing with a system that makes life harder rather than easier for decision makers can be high, for ineffectiveness and inefficiency are wasteful of the organization's resources.

The fundamental aspects of complexity with which an organization must deal are decomposability of systems, evolution from the simple and given to the complex and unmapped, the need for feedback and redundant arrangements to facilitate learning, and the requirements of levels for specific, task-related information. These aspects point to certain considerations that should not be ignored by the MIS: A MIS should aim to aid decision makers at specific levels rather than at the level of the system. It should aim to aid decision makers in areas where knowledge of the important variables and agreement of procedure are relatively secure. It should incorporate deliberate overlapping and duplicate arrangements with short feedback spans. It should produce data that relate to tasks and objectives at narrow levels. The key to resolving complexity lies in linkages. Any potential resolution must deal with breaking a system into linked units and then mapping these units appropriately, if utility is to obtain.

FAILURE TO MAKE THE RIGHT TRADEOFFS

Failure to make the right tradeoffs deprives an organization of the capacity to deal adequately with complexity. Management information systems fail because of major confusion in conceptual foundations. Too many organizations struggle to relate what goes into the system to what comes out of the system — to relate storage to retrieval — while failing entirely to relate the system to specific referents in the real world of policy problems and decisions.

REFERENCES

ACKOFF, R. L. (1967) "Management information systems." Management Science 14, 4: 147-156.
ANAND, H. (1971) "A computer-based hospital information system." Hospital Administration in Canada 13 (September): 46-51.
ASHBY, W. R. (1961) Introduction to Cybernetics. London: Chapman & Hall.
CYERT, R. M. and J. G. MARCH (1966a) A Behavioral Theory of the Firm. Englewood Cliffs, NJ: Prentice-Hall.
——— (1966b) "Basic concepts," in Selections from A Behavioral Theory of the Firm. Englewood Cliffs, NJ: Prentice-Hall.
DANZIGER, J. N. (n.d.) "Computers, local government and the litany to EDP." Public Policy Research Organization, University of California, Irvine. (unpublished)
EMERY, J. C. (1967) "Economics of information," pp. 158-167 in Ideas for Management, Papers and Case Histories Presented at the 1967 International Systems Meeting, Systems and Procedures Association of America.
GARRETT, R. C. (1973) Hospitals: A Systems Approach. Philadelphia: Auerbach.
GORDON, P. J. (1961-1962) "The top management triangle in voluntary hospitals, parts I and II." Journal of the Academy of Management 4/5: 205-214/66-75.
GORRY, G. A. and M. J. S. MORTON (1971) "A framework for management information systems." Sloan Management Review 13, 1: 55-70.
HEYDEBRAND, W. (1975) Hospital Bureaucracy. Englewood Cliffs, NJ: Prentice-Hall.
HOWLAND, D. (1961) The Development of a Methodology for Evaluating Patient Care. Columbus: Ohio State University Press.
KNIGHT, F. H. (1964) Risk, Uncertainty and Profit. New York: A. M. Kelley.
LANDAU, M. (1973) "On the concept of a self-correcting organization." Public Administration Review 33, 6: 33-42.
——— (1969) "Redundancy, rationality, and the problems of duplication and overlap." Public Administration Review 29, 4: 346-356.
MARCH, J. and H. E. SIMON (1959) "Conflict in organizations," pp. 124-129 in Organizations. New York: John Wiley.

177

MEIR, R. L. (1961) "Information input overload: features of growth in communications-oriented institutions." Presented at the Colloquium on the Economics of Information, American Association for the Advancement of Science, December 26.

MINTZBERG, H. (1973) The Nature of Managerial Work. New York: Harper & Row.

NEWELL, A. (1969) "Heuristic programming: ill-structured problems," in J. Aronofsky (ed.) Publications in Operations Research 16. New York: John Wiley.

OLSON, M. (1971) The Logic of Collective Action, Public Goods and the Theory of Groups. Cambridge, MA: Harvard University Press.

RITTEL, H. and M. WEBBER (1973) " Dilemma in the general theory of planning." Policy Sciences 4: 155-169.

SIMON, H. (1969) The Sciences of the Artificial. Boston: MIT Press.

——— (1960) The New Science of Management Decision. New York: Harper & Row.

——— (1957) "A behavioral model of rational choice," pp. 241-260 in H. A. Simon, Models of Management. New York: John Wiley.

———, H. GUETZKOW, G. KOZMETSKY, and G. TYNDALL (1954) Centralization vs. Decentralization in Organizing the Controller's Department. Pittsburgh: Carnegie Institute of Technology.

STRAUSS, A. L. SCHATZMAN, D. EHRLICH, R. BUCHER, and M. SABSHIN (1971) "The hospital and its negotiation order," pp. 147-169 in E. Friedson (ed.) The Hospital in Modern Society. New York: Free Press.

TROW, M. (1975) "The public and private lives of higher education." Daedalus 2 (Winter): 113-127.

TVERSKY, A. and D. KAHNEMAN (1974) "Judgement under uncertainty: hueristics and biases." Science 185: 1124-1131.

WEICK, K. E. (1976) "Education organizations as loosely coupled systems." Administrative Science Quarterly 21: 1-19.

——— (1969) The Social Psychology of Organizing. Reading, MA: Addison-Wesley.

WILDAVSKY, A. (1979) "Policy as its own cause," pp. 62-85 in Speaking Truth to Power. Boston: Little, Brown.

——— (1977) "Doing better and feeling worse: the political pathology of health policy." Daedalus (Winter).

——— (1974) The Politics of the Budgetary Process. Boston: Little, Brown.

——— and J. YUROW (1979) "Information as an organizational problem." Prepared for the National Telecommunications and Information Administration, U.S. Department of Commerce. (unpublished)

INDEX

180   Simple Systems, Complex Environments

Board of directors, 127, 128, 147; and
   organizational goals, 25, 26; errors
   encountered by, 99 (table); effects of
   error on, 100, 103; evaluation by, 164,
   168, 172-173
Bootlegging, 105-106
Budget, 48, 61-62, 91, 100, 102, 103, 133,
   135, 153, 162, 163-164, 170
Business management, 17
Bypassing, 104

Care, quality of, 22, 28, 39, 125, 127
Case knowledge, 144
Change, 32, 44, 72, 74, 90, 91, 116, 117,
   121-122, 152-153, 159-160, 164
Charge reports, 61, 63, 64, 65 (table), 66
Charges, 59-60, 77, 81, 88, 94,112-113,
   162
Claim settlement, 57, 80-81
Coding, 74, 78, 83, 93, 98, 104, 107,
   109-110
Competition, 41-42. See also
   Interorganizational status
   competition
Complexity, 17-18, 28-29; and data
   production, 46, 47, 52-54; from
   external requirements, 76-77; and
   interconnected subsystems, 92; as
   problem, 154-155; and MIS, 155,
   156 (table), 157, 159, 165-167, 168,
   174-175; response to, 155-159,
   165 (table); evolution of, 159-160; and
   tradeoffs, 167-175
Comprehensiveness, 88, 168-169
Compromise, 144. See also Negotiation
Concentrated interests, 60-61
Conflict, 33-34, 150-151, 157, 164, 165; in
   management by exception, 73, 75-76;
   and errors, 100, 102
Consultants, 128, 162
Consumers. See Users
Control, 89, 98, 103, 108, 113-117 passim,
   146, 147, 158, 160, 164, 165, 169.
   See also Cost-control
Coordination, 164-165, 169-170; and
   behavioral/informational
   relationships, 32; and
   professionalism, 33;
   by multipurpose systems, 80

Coping, 104-108, 105 (table)
Correction, 110, 113-114
Cost-control 20-21, 24, 28-29, 161-162
Cost of data/information, 20, 45-46, 54,
   60-61, 64, 66-67, 70-76 passim, 80, 89,
   91-92, 93, 145-146, 167-168, 170-171,
   174; externalization of, 61, 66-67, 171
Cost of health care, 70, 81, 86, 112, 122,
   123-124
Crisis, 35, 86-88, 98, 108
Cross-training, 53-54
Cumulativity, 88
Cyert, Richard M., 33-34, 168

Danziger, James N., 145-146
Data: and complexity, 17-18, 52-54,
   76-77, 165-167; and external
   environment, 19; and public/private
   aims, 19-20, 21-22, 30; and MIS
   design, 27-28; flow of, 31-32; and
   exchange relationship, 42;
   production of, 45-47, 169-171;
   expense of, 60-61, 64, 66-67;
   production of, v. collective good,
   60-64; procurement of, 65 (table);
   integration of, 69-71, 79; filtered, 71,
   73-76, 85, 103, 136, 141;
   overabundance of, 71-72, 91, 153, 155,
   157, 166-167; and
   multipurposefulness, 80, 82, 94; and
   inadequate reports, 88, 89; and
   interconnected subsystems, 91-93;
   overdistribution of, 93-94; effects of
   error on, 100, 103, 104; poor quality
   of, 108-113, 117, 119, 137-138, 157-159;
   conversion of, into information, 116;
   and program evaluation, 137-139,
   163-165; relevance of, 163-165, 172,
   173; and priorities, 169
Data base, 146, 159, 162; accuracy of,
   70-71; pool approach to, 71-72, 90;
   sequential processing of, 74; and
   exceptions, 75; linkages in, 79
Data-processing (DP), 55, 56, 72, 76, 79,
   93, 94, 123, 126
Debt write-off, 101, 103, 132
Decision-making: and public/private
   aims, 19-20; and organizational
   actors, 25-26; and appropriate data,

Garrett, Raymon D., 25
Generality v. power, 142-146, 143 (fig.),
    145 (fig.), 167-168
Geriatrics Department, 72
Goals: valuation of, 23-24; multiple,
    24-27, 28-29, 137, 141; conflict over,
    33-34, 150-151, 157; administrative
    responsibility for, 127, 128, 131, 139;
    management of, 171
Gordon, P. J., 36
Gorry, G. Anthony, 173
Government agencies, 18-21 passim, 26,
    28, 29, 30, 57, 72, 78, 81, 128

Heydebrand, Wolf, 33
Hidden costs, 145-146

Incremental decision, 151 (fig.), 152
Informal communication network,
    38-40, 77, 78, 127, 130, 137, 164
Information: and public/private aims,
    19-20; as incentive for data
    production, 61-62; and exception
    power, 75; and patient record, 77-79;
    necessary characteristics of, 89-90;
    undersupply of, 91; adaptation of,
    97-98, 102, 104-106, 170-171;
    conversion of data into, 116; types
    needed, 120; inadequacies in, 123;
    and administrative requirements,
    130-133; dissemination of, 133-134;
    and management problems, 136-140;
    usefulness of, 146; analysis of, 153
Informational relationships, 31-32
Informational systems, 69-70; total,
    70-71. See also Management
    information system
Input, 45, 70, 84, 89, 92, 116; serial,
    27-28; and error response, 105
    (table); evaluation of, 139
Insurance companies, 18, 86; and
    reports, 80; and amended bills, 84
Insurance data, 49-52 passim, 65 (table),
    94
Integration of data, 69-71, 79
Intelligence-gathering network, 104,
    127, 130
Interconnection of subsystems, 91-93,
    111-112, 154-155, 166, 168-169

Interorganizational status competition,
    46-47, 49-52
Intuition, 98, 104, 144, 148, 172
Irrational environment, 114-115

Job description, 72

Knowledge, 115-117, 155, 159; and
    decision-making, 142, 143, 144,
    152-153, 158, 167, 168; and action, 149

Laboratory, 47, 60, 133
Laboratory Technology Department, 37
Landau, Martin, 114-115, 116, 149, 150,
    151
Learning, 116, 160
Levels, organizational, 166-167; and data
    production, 47, 54-58; and data
    expense, 66; and faulty data, 112; and
    information problems, 136; and
    management function, 171-174
Linkages, 79, 155, 174

Management by exception, 71, 73-76,
    80-81, 86, 94, 145, 167-168
Management information system (MIS):
    and complexity, 17-18, 155, 156 (fig.),
    157, 159, 165-167, 168, 174-175; design
    of, 27-30, 32, 44, 71-76, 79-82, 90-94;
    and data production, 45, 51, 52, 67;
    and departmental status, 66;
    multipurpose, 79-82, 94; as solution,
    90; as problem, 90-94, 115, 161-163; as
    cause of error, 97-98; and error
    control, 113-114, 116-117; as planning
    tool, 119, 121; as administrative aid,
    132-133; and program evaluation,
    137-139; and meaningful data, 141;
    problem-solving capabilities of,
    145-146, 152; anticipated benefits of,
    163-165
Managers, 162; and data production, 53,
    61-62; and overabundant data, 71-72;
    and filtered data, 73-74, 75; and
    reports, 80; data needs of, 90, 91, 92,
    94; and crisis, 98; errors encountered
    by, 99 (table); effects of error on, 100,
    102-103; and financial operations,
    122-126; information problems of,

Values, 169; and data production, 67; v. facts, 151 (fig.), 152-153, 160. *See also* Dual value system

Webber, Melvin, 142
Weick, Karl E., 114, 149-150
Wildavsky, Aaron, 23-24, 134, 141
Workload, 51, 54, 63, 85, 86-87, 88, 124, 132, 133

ABOUT THE AUTHOR

Mari Malvey was my student and my friend. She died in a car crash with her son Nicky while on her way to meet me to begin a coauthored book on information systems. She was 44 years old. My personal and professional loss are beyond expression.

Mari Malvey was an Assistant Professor in the Department of Business and Administrative Studies at Lewis and Clark College in Portland, Oregon. She taught courses and did consulting on management information systems. Before this she was a graduate student in the Political Science Department of the University of California at Berkeley. During her time there she taught in the Division of Interdisciplinary Studies, where she had a devoted corps of students who respected her extraordinarily wide-ranging knowledge of history and comparative politics. Among other things, she spoke French, Greek, and Russian fluently. She cared for her students and they reciprocated by doing better work than they thought they could. Mari knew what that was about. She surmounted many more difficulties than most of us to become a scholar and teacher.

The virtues exemplified in this book — combining theoretical understanding with practical experience and personal empathy for the problems of the people involved — were enriched in the last several years with Mari's broader view of her subject. She taught herself computing and programming. The secret lives of data designers and processors were opened up to her. She was ready to express an enlarged conception of the problems of converting data into information within an organizational context.

Now none of this can be. Only those who knew her can gauge the loss of her contribution. It would be unsuited to Mari's character to leave her with a lament. Her gaiety was an inseparable part of her life. She knew how to pick herself up, put herself together, make a wry comment about the inscrutable ways of providence, and get on with it.

                                                                    — AW